# Playing Out of Your Mind
## A Soccer Player and Coaches Guide to Developing Mental Toughness

### by Dr. Alan Goldberg

Published by
REEDSWAIN INC

## Library of Congress Cataloging - in - Publication Data

Goldberg, Dr. Alan
  Playing Out of Your Mind/Dr. Alan Goldberg

ISBN No. 1-59164-165-9
Library of Congress Control Number - 2012935789
Copyright © 1997

Reedswain books are available at special discounts for bulk purchase. For details, contact the Special Sales Manager at Reedswain by calling 1-800-331-5191.

Printed in the United States of America.

Credits: Art Direction, Layout and Cover Design - Kimberly N. Bender
Cover Photo: EMPICS

REEDSWAIN, INC.
88 Wells Road • Spring City PA 19475
1-800-331-5191
Web Site: www.reedswain.com

# Table of Contents

# Introduction

## What It Takes to Become a Champion

There is absolutely no question that soccer is an intensely physical sport. To excel you must not only have a high degree of ballhandling skills and knowledge of the game's strategies, but also tremendous endurance, good footwork and physical strength. Without consistent and proper training in these physical aspects of the game you can never become a champion.

Unfortunately, most athletes playing the game today stop their training at this point. They make a critical mistake in assuming that all you need to play the game well are the above mentioned physical attributes. Consequently, they leave one of the **MOST IMPORTANT** parts of the game to chance, the mental side! There is **FAR** more to a soccer match than kicking, trapping, tackling, or marking your man. You have to be able to use your head! And I am **NOT** talking about headers!!

When a striker beats his defender, breaks free on a solo run and misses an easy shot on goal this is **NOT** because of a lack of skills. When the best players in the world miss penalty kicks, this is **NOT** because of a lack of training! When a team that should easily win gets upset by a much weaker opponent, this can NOT be explained away by talking about the physical prowess of the victors! When you play below your potential because you are intimidated or psyched out, this is **NOT** because you have suddenly lost your ball handling skills! These examples **all** reflect the mental side of the game, the **PSYCHOLOGICAL DIMENSION**.

The great players in this game not only have the physical skills, conditioning and technical smarts, they also have the right "head" for the game. In other words, they are mentally tough. Either directly or indirectly they have trained themselves to excel in this psychological dimension. If you have ever choked, missed easy shots, gotten totally intimidated by an opponent or played poorly because you lacked confidence or had your head filled with negativity, then you **KNOW** exactly what I am talking about when I discuss the mental side of your game.

To become a champion you must start to systematically train this mental side, your "inner-player". You must take a little bit of time to learn to handle competitive pressures, concentrate and block out distractions, rebound quickly from setbacks and bad breaks, develop confidence, avoid psyche-outs and intimidation, and learn to think and act like a winner. These are the mental skills displayed by winners! You can learn them too!

If you truly want to become the best player that you can be, to gain that **COMPETITIVE EDGE** over the competition, then you must start **TODAY** to develop the mind of a champion. Mental toughness will lift your level of play several notches. It will help you hold your own even with more physically talented or skilled players. However, if you leave the mental side of your game to chance, if you never learn how to handle big game pressure, if you concentrate on the wrong things before and during the game, or if you never learn how to effectively let go of mistakes and bad breaks, then all of your ability, hard work, and good coaching gets wasted.

To be a winner you must balance your training. You must train your inner as well as your outer game. This book was designed to help you directly develop the mental skills that will help you maximize your physical potential. If **YOU** want, **YOU** can develop the mind of a champion. All it takes is a little extra effort both on and off the pitch. A little extra practice time is a very small price to pay in order to be able to better handle big game pressures. It is a small price to pay if it helps you learn to control the negative thoughts or emotions which threaten to get you red carded.

# Why Soccer Players Fail To Develop Mental Toughness

First let us get the unpleasantness out of the way. Let me tell you why this book will not work for you. The biggest mistake that athletes make with mental training is they fail to practice it properly. They hear about techniques that help you think like a winner or stay calm under pressure, but they **FAIL** to practice these techniques properly. If you read this book without taking time to work on the exercises you will not get as much as you can from it. Sure, you will get a few great ideas that will probably lift your level of play a bit. **BUT**, if you are really serious about becoming a champion and taking your game as high as it can go, then you must take the time to develop these **SKILLS**.

Mental skills are no different than ball handling skills in that you must practice both in order to excel. If you never practice controlling the ball with one touch, then you can not expect yourself to perform that skill in a pressured game situation. Similarly, if you never practice techniques for concentrating and blocking out distractions, you will **NOT** be able to stay focused under pressure. **MENTAL SKILLS MUST BE PRACTICED FIRST IN A NON-STRESSFUL ENVIRONMENT BEFORE YOU CAN DEPEND ON THEM TO WORK FOR YOU IN THE HIGH STRESS OF A BIG GAME!**

Proper practice means that you must spend time with these mental skills on a regular basis. Ten to thirty minutes a day is all it takes for you to begin to excel mentally on the pitch. Furthermore you must be patient. Give yourself enough time with each of these skills to learn them. If you rush through these exercises or get frustrated because they do not work right away you will be robbing yourself of the chance to truly develop as a player.

Remember, the best players and coaches in the game today actively use their mental skills to dominate play. Anson Dorrance, Women's Soccer Coach at the University of North Carolina, Chapel Hill and Coach of the 1991 Women's World Cup Champions, is so successful because he is a master of training this psychological dimension. On a daily basis, in every practice, Anson teaches his players how to be mentally tough.

# Do Not Re-Invent The Wheel

This book is based on an important operating principle of peak performance and success: **IF IT IS POSSIBLE FOR ONE PERSON IN THE WORLD TO DO SOMETHING THEN IT IS POSSIBLE FOR YOU**. If someone excels tremendously in this game then it is possible for you to reach a comparable level of success. All that is missing is the **HOW**. What I mean by this is that if you can find out the **STRATEGIES** which successful players use, i.e. how they train, how they handle pressure, how they deal with bad breaks and setbacks, how they maintain motivation, etc., and if you start to regularly use these strategies, then you too can dramatically improve your game!

Just because you study and use all of the training strategies of a Tab Ramos, Michelle Ackers Stahl, Tony Meola or Cara Jennings does not mean that you will be able to play as well as them. However, the "lie" that I am presenting as an operating principle is a good "lie" to organize your life around.

Let me explain.

If you find out the success strategies of all of the great players, what they do physically, mentally, how they eat, etc., and you start to practice just like them, you will lift your level of play tremendously. If you act as if this principle were true, then you will achieve far more as a soccer player than you would otherwise. **DO NOT RE-INVENT THE WHEEL**. Study the great players and learn from them. If you are really daring I suggest you even call them up and talk to them. Most will be more than happy to help you. **DO NOT TRAIN OR COACH IN A VACUUM**. If you are open to learning you will improve quickly and be more successful than if you think you have all the answers. Talk to, read about and study the experts. It is one of the fastest ways you can improve.

That is exactly where the exercises in this book come from, the experts! Not me! I have stolen **EVERYTHING** in this book from great athletes and coaches. All you need to do is **TAKE ACTION** and **USE** them!

# You Have a Super Athlete Inside

As a soccer player you have tremendous potential. You have hidden resources. You have the ability to do things you never imagined! Now whether you believe this or not, it is true. Motivational speakers across the country throw around statistics like, "you only realize 5% of your potential" or "you have 50 times more ability than you think you do." Personally, I have no idea how much of your potential you are using or if you have 20, 40, or 50 times more ability than you think. What I do **KNOW** from my work with athletes and other performers outside of sports is that you are **NOT** operating on all your cylinders! You do **NOT** know what your limits are, nor how much you can achieve.

I have seen the impossible accomplished too many times to really believe that most limits can not be broken. Roger Bannister's sub-four minute mile blew the lid off that theory back in 1954. Mike Powell recently broke Bob Beamon's long jump record, another impossible task. A kid named Dick Fosbury set a world record and won a gold medal at the '68 Mexico City Olympics by going over the high jump bar backwards! Jim Abbott, pitching Phenom for the California Angles does not have a right hand! The wonders of your limitless ability are all around you. There is little that you cannot achieve if you have the right **STRATEGIES**, are **MOTIVATED** to succeed, and are **PERSISTENT**. The only real limits that exist out there are the ones you have in your mind. When you overcome those inner limits you will start doing the impossible.

# Chapter 1: The Mind Body Connection

## All Performance is Self-Fulfilling

One of the first things you must understand if you are going to develop the mind of a champion is the idea that **ALL PERFORMANCE IS SELF-FULFILLING**. What I mean by this is that **YOU GET WHAT YOU EXPECT AS A PLAYER**. If you go into a game expecting to play like garbage, you will play like garbage. If you go in expecting to have fun and play strongly, you will! This is because of the Mind-Body connection.

If you go into a game situation and you are telling yourself things like, "These guys are so good...I feel lousy...Last game I really played badly, what if I can not control the ball again", etc. This is what is beginning to happen inside your body: Your muscles are beginning to tighten up, your breathing is becoming faster and shallower, your heart and pulse rate are increasing and you are beginning to lose circulation in your hands and feet. The end result, performance-wise, of all these physical changes are: your reflexes and foot speed slow down, (tight muscles will do this **EVERY** time), your movements become less fluid and more awkward, (tight muscles again), you lose your feel of the ball, (from the loss of circulation in your feet), and your endurance suffers, (shallow and rapid breathing will kill your wind no matter what kind of good physical shape you are in!).

The difference between your **BEST** and Worst games (if you have paid your physical dues, you are in shape, know the skills and strategies, etc.) is "upstairs", it is mental and has to do with what you think, say to yourself and imagine, **BEFORE**, **DURING** and **AFTER** you play. Your **MENTAL STRATEGIES**, (thoughts, self-talk and images) before your best games are very different than the ones that you use before your **WORST** ones.

## Discovering Your "Inner Coach"

### Exercise #1 • Reviewing Past Peak Performances

Find yourself a quiet place, free from distractions. Think about the last time you had an awesome game, the last time you really felt great as a player, either for part of the game or the entire game. With your eyes closed, use your imagination right now to go back in time to this game and see, hear and feel everything that went on in this match that made it so special. **FIRST**, focus on what was occurring **BEFORE** the game started. What were you thinking? What was the voice of your "inner coach" saying to you about the match? Were you looking forward to it or not? Did you involve any imagery before the game? What were you concentrating on? **SECOND**, what was going on mentally **DURING** the game? What kind of self-talk were you aware of? If you made a mistake, were beaten by an opponent or tackled hard, how did you deal with it mentally? What did you say to yourself about these mistakes? **THIRD**, what went on mentally after the match ended? How did you feel?

## Exercise #2 • Reviewing Past Bad Performances

Sit quietly and comfortably in a place that is free from distractions. Now I would like you to do something a little less pleasant. Think about the last time you had an awful game, the last time you went onto the pitch and were really disappointed with your play. Close your eyes and turn on that VCR in your mind's eye. I want you to go back in time and see, hear and feel everything you did when you were at this game. **FIRST**, focus in on what was going on mentally **BEFORE** the game started. What kind of expectations did you have? What was your pre-game self-talk like? Were you dreading the match? What kind of imagery did you entertain, if any? What were you focusing on? **SECOND**, what was going on mentally **DURING** the game? What kind of self-talk did you have? What were you focusing on? How did you deal with mistakes and bad breaks? If you were beaten by another player or missed an easy shot how did you handle this mentally? **THIRD**, what happened after the game? What did you say to yourself? What kind of feelings did you generate inside?

If you spend a little time with these two exercises examining both your good and bad games you will soon see **HOW** your play is directly related to **WHAT** you think, before and during the game. Often games are won and lost **BEFORE** they even start. How often have you mentally taken yourself out of a game before the opening whistle because you got psyched out by the other team, another player or the size of the crowd?

## Exercise #3 • Comparing Good and Bad Performances

Take five minutes or so with a pen and paper to jot down what you just discovered to be the mental differences between good and bad games. Make a list of the self-talk you were aware of before and during the good game. Then do the same thing for the self-talk related to the bad game. Now compare the two. If you want, you might find it useful to examine several good and bad games. You should begin to see a pattern develop.

This first series of exercises should help you understand that good and bad performances are **NOT** random, but are **DIRECTLY** related to your mindset. If you go into a match feeding yourself negativity and mental garbage your play will reflect this. When you make mistakes or things do not go your way you will have a tendency to hang onto these mistakes and bring yourself down further. Conversely, if you go into the game with positive self-talk and optimistic thoughts, you will perform much closer to your potential. You will quickly rebound from bad breaks or mistakes and they will have no adverse effect on your play.

These exercises are important because they will provide you with an awareness of your before, and during game mental strategies, (thoughts, self-talk and imagery). It is this awareness that will help you make the necessary changes to become a mentally tough player. Without an awareness you will **NOT** be able to change negative or self defeating thoughts or behaviors. You will, instead, be a victim to them.

**AWARENESS IS THE KEY TO CHANGE.** If you are having trouble controlling the ball with one touch, change and improvement will only happen **AFTER** you become aware of exactly what you are doing wrong. Once you can feel, see, and understand the mistake, you are then in a position to correct it. This same principle operates mentally. You must **FIRST** get to know your negative, performance related thought patterns before you can change them. If you do not play to your potential against certain teams or opponents you must become aware of how you mentally sabotage yourself in these situations before you can correct the problem.

As a player, it is critical that you do not underestimate the power of your "inner coach", i.e. your self-talk, in effecting how well you play. I would like to demonstrate this to you with the following exercise:

## Exercise #4 • The Power of The Mind and the Body Connection

Find yourself a space that is free from distractions. Stand with your feet shoulder width apart and arms resting comfortably at your sides. Understand that this is an exercise to test how well you use your imagination. Raise your arms so that they are perpendicular to your body at shoulder height and your palms are facing each other. Take your left palm and turn it up towards the ceiling. Take your right thumb and stick it up in the air. **CLOSE YOUR EYES AND, USING YOUR IMAGINATION ONLY,** imagine that in your left hand you have a very heavy book. Imagine that attached to your right thumb is a string which is connected to a balloon filled with helium.

Using **ONLY** your imagination, imagine that your left hand is getting heavier, and heavier, and falling...and that your right hand is getting lighter and lighter and rising. Allow yourself enough time with each of these suggestions so that you begin to imagine them actually happening. Repeat these suggestions of heaviness and lightness to yourself for 1-2 minutes. Now open your eyes, look at both arms and see if you can notice a difference in the physical feelings in each. If you really let your imagination run free, chances are that you saw and felt a difference. The left arm probably felt heavier and more fatigued than the right one.

# The G.I.G.O. Factor

If you did experience feelings of fatigue and tension in your left arm, understand that these feelings were very **REAL**. The thing that was in your imagination was the book. This exercise highlights how the thoughts and self-talk which you entertain in your head go directly into your body and make physical changes that effect your performance. For example, if you are telling yourself in the middle of the second half that you are too tired to hang in there, that you are totally exhausted, these self suggestions will make you feel even more tired. If you focus on a defender before the game and tell yourself how skillful and fast he is and how slow you are, you will be slower than normal that game.

This is what I call the **GIGO** factor. **GIGO** is an acronym taken from computer terminology and it stands for Garbage In, Garbage Out. If you program garbage into a computer, i.e. the wrong instructions, it will give you garbage back out. If you program garbage into **YOUR** computer, i.e. your brain, the garbage which results is your poor performance. You are set to take a penalty kick and the outcome of the game rests on **YOUR** foot. Before the shot all you can think about is, "what if I miss...last week I kicked it right to the keeper.. I am so nervous", etc. This focus of concentration is the Garbage In. The Garbage Out results in tight muscles, low confidence and a ball that goes over the crossbars and into another zip code!

Your **SELF SUGGESTIONS** will not only have a powerful impact on how well you play, but how your team performs. Teams get into slumps and fall apart because of the **GIGO** factor. In 1987 I worked with the University of Massachusetts women's soccer team during the NCAA Division I tournament. The U. Mass. women had gotten to the Final Four 5 years in a row and lost each time in the first game. The team's self suggestion floating around was "we can not win the big game." Until you and your teammates change those negative messages you will not be able to change how you play!

## REMEMBER, PERFORMANCE IS SELF FULFILLING....YOU GET WHAT YOU EXPECT.

If you tell yourself you "can not" do something, or "this always happens to me", then do not be surprised if you are right! It is critical that your self suggestions and "inner coachings" are positive. Instead of garbage in, garbage out, you want Good Stuff in and Good Stuff out! To get you started on this process, keep a daily performance journal.

# Performance Journal

Start to log all your thoughts, self talk, feelings and attitudes before, during and after you practice and play. **DO NOT DO THIS EXERCISE WHILE**

**YOU ARE PRACTICING OR COMPETING**. Log these thoughts at night when you can really concentrate on them.

The purpose of this exercise is to help you become more aware. Try to capture the exact words, phrases and even the voice tones that you use on yourself. Not only will the journal help you to begin to develop an awareness of any negative thought patterns, but just the process of paying attention to, and recording these thoughts will help you begin to eliminate them.

# Chapter 2:
# Five Steps to Becoming a Champion

I want to provide you a road map for becoming a winner. Follow it closely and I **GUARANTEE** your performance level will rise several notches. Ignore it and your successes will be few and far between. These 5 strategies belong to hundreds of world class and Olympic level athletes across every sport. All you need to do is read and follow them closely.

## #1 Start with the End in Mind • Have a Dream

If you want to be as good a player as possible you have to **BE SMART** about your training. This means simply that you must have a clear goal or direction. You have to know where you want to go in order to get there. As a competitive tennis player I unknowingly limited my potential because, despite the fact that I worked hard and trained every day, I had no direction. I had no big dream, nor any goals that were useful to me. I just put my time in.

Most successful athletes begin their careers with a dream. Sometimes that dream is so big and so unrealistic that they are too embarrassed to share it with anyone because they are afraid they will be ridiculed. A dream will give your life a focus in which you can channel your energies. A dream or goal will provide you with the motivation to persist in the face of obstacles and defeat. A dream will draw you like a magnet towards it's achievement.

One of the first steps in becoming a champion is to use your imagination! You create your own reality. Start by using your imagination to think about how far you want to go in this sport. Do you want to play on the national team? Do you want to play Division I ball and have a college scholarship? Do you want to go all the way and play on a World Cup Team or compete professionally? **EVERY** great achievement starts with a shaky thought or fantasy. The more you dwell on this fantasy the more it begins to take shape and become more real to you.

## Remember . . . Anything You Can Conceive of (Dream), and Believe in, You Can Achieve

Motivation is all about having a big enough **WHY**. Why are you training? Why do you want to put all that time in? Why are you sacrificing and giving up other more enjoyable things for soccer? If you have a big enough **WHY**, you can accomplish anything! So the question to ask yourself is what is your **WHY**? What is your soccer dream?

Sure, I know what happens when you let your imagination run away with these questions. There is a little voice that raises its ugly little head and starts to put you down, or ridicule you for being so stupid to think that you would even dream you could accomplish **THAT**. Humor yourself right now! Suspend judgment and disbelief. Think about your dream, what are your soccer goals? But **START WITH THE END IN MIND**.

# Step #1 • Your Future Athlete

Sit quietly in a room where you will be undisturbed for the next 15-20 minutes. Have your arms and legs uncrossed and close your eyes. Take a few minutes to relax yourself as much as possible. Focus on your breathing. Take yourself to a relaxing place or otherwise calm yourself as best you can. Now briefly think about your ultimate goal or dream as a soccer player. If you could create a movie in which you would be the star, where would you be? How far have you gone in your career? Try to be as specific as possible and **REMEMBER**, suspend any and all judgments about the reality of this actually happening.

Let those thoughts briefly fade and go to a very relaxing place which we will call your **RESOURCE PLACE**. You can create this place in your imagination or you can mentally return to a special beach, lake, mountain or place that you have been to before. See, hear and feel everything that you would if you actually were in this special place. Try to fill in the details of the scene, the sights, movements, colors, lighting, sounds etc..

**NEXT**, imagine that you are watching your **FUTURE SELF** in this place, becoming a great soccer player. Imagine that you can watch a great player play in front of you. What does he look like? How does he carry himself? What does he sound like?

**NEXT**, imagine that you can watch him begin to handle the ball. Study very carefully what he does. His ball control, touch, ballhandling skills and speed. Watch him as he practices or even plays in a game, but do so by carefully taking note of everything he does. Watch his defense skills. Watch how he moves away with the ball. If he is in goal watch and listen to him controlling the action or leading the team.

**NEXT**, imagine that you can float up out of your body on the sidelines and float right into his body so that you become the great soccer player in your imagination. Now you want to pretend that you are him. You can associate and identify with this great soccer player. You can see, hear and feel what he would. If you were this player right now, what would you believe to be true about yourself and your abilities? Now, as you are imagining you are this great player, spend some time on the pitch playing just the way that you saw him performing. Feel what it is like to control your body and the ball the way he does. Carry the exercise over to playing in a big game. See, hear and feel yourself, as this **FUTURE SELF** player on the pitch, in the game.

Spend 10 minutes a night with this exercise before you go to sleep, imagining that you are living your dream. It has been said that your imagination rules your world. This is a constructive way to take control of that world. Regular practice of this exercise will help you get one step closer to turning your dream into a reality.

## Motivation from Goal Setting that Really Works

What is the best way for you to move towards that dream? And how can you keep yourself motivated through the long- haul?

First understand that **MOTIVATION IS A PERSONAL THING. IT IS UP TO YOU!!!** You can not depend on other people to get you motivated. Sure, coaches, parents and other players can help steer you in the right direction. But it is up to you to do the actual work. This is why it is important for you to have a big goal that is really worth working and sacrificing for.

## Eating Elephants

However, you can not stop here. If all you have is a big dream, and you do not ground that dream in the day to day reality of practice, you will not go anywhere. One of the biggest mistakes athletes make around goal setting is to pick out a huge, faraway goal for themselves, i.e. "I want to make the National Team", and then forget about it. If you want to be successful and have the motivation to keep going you must figure out a way to take your ultimate goal and break it down into smaller and smaller pieces.

In other words, **YOU MUST TAKE YOUR DREAM AND BREAK IT DOWN INTO YEARLY, 6 MONTH, MONTHLY, WEEKLY, AND ESPECIALLY DAILY GOALS, IN ORDER TO MAKE IT HAPPEN!**

This is known as the "eat an elephant" strategy. The only smart way to eat an elephant is to break it down into bite size pieces. You eat an elephant one bite at a time. If you try to shove an entire leg into your mouth at one time you will get a bad case of crushing indigestion. So too with that big dream. If you constantly focus on how far away it is, and **ALL** that you have to do to accomplish it, you will get mental indigestion, i.e. you will get **DISCOURAGED** and lose your motivation.

It is the accumulation of very small successes on a daily and weekly basis that fuels your motivation and keeps you going. It is the idea that: **INCH BY INCH ANYTHING IS A CINCH, YARD BY YARD IT MIGHT BE HARD!**

Understand also that your goals should function like a road map to help you start your journey, keep you on track, and insure that you end up where you were heading. Therefore you want to be smart about those goals.

## First Assess Where you are Right Now!

If your goal is to play soccer at a Division I school, and you are a freshman in high school, start by honestly assessing your **STRENGTHS** and **WEAK-**

**NESSES** in every aspect of the game. Look at your ballhandling skills, endurance, knowledge of the game, physical speed, strength, mental toughness, etc. Consult with your coach or someone who really knows you and the game. Be open and honest with yourself. You cannot get better unless you first acknowledge your weaknesses.

# Next Find Out What Skills are Needed to Reach Your Goal

What do the scholarship soccer players at Division I schools have that you do not? What are the skills and strengths that are necessary to play at this level? Talk to your coach, college coaches and even college players on these teams to help you with the answers. And remember about asking the experts!! If you do have an opportunity to talk to some of these players, find out exactly how they did it. What was the road they took?

Knowing where you are **NOW**, and what you **SPECIFICALLY** need to work on to reach your dream, will provide you with a very clear path to follow toward success. Once you have this path outlined, all you need to do is follow it! It is similar to using the 1-10 exercise.

**ON A SCALE OF 1 - 10, WHERE 1 = YOU ARE THE WORST SOCCER PLAYER IN THE WORLD AND 10 = YOU ARE THE PLAYER WHO HAS REACHED HIS GOAL. WHERE ARE YOU? COME UP WITH A NUMBER. NOW, IF YOU COME UP WITH A 4 OR 5, WHAT DO YOU SPECIFICALLY NEED TO WORK ON TO RAISE YOUR NUMBER TO 10.**

Your success starts with your ability to **DREAM**. Dream big! Have big scary goals. **BUT**, if you are going to build your castles in the sky, **MAKE SURE THE FOUNDATION OF THAT CASTLE IS ON THE GROUND!** In other words, you must tie your big goal to your daily, in practice goals, for the whole process to really work for you. If you can connect what you are doing in practice **TODAY** to your goal which is 3 or 4 years away, you will get much more out of practice and will maintain a high degree of motivation.

For example, a very talented figure skater was having trouble dragging herself out of bed every morning at 4 am to train in an ice cold rink for 2 hours before school. After missing several practices she came up with a way to get beyond the day-to-day discomfort of having to leave that warm bed. She found a photograph of the top Romanian skater she knew she would be facing in the next World Championships and put the picture by her bedside. Under the photo she wrote the following words: "Comrade, while you were sleeping, I was training." This was all that she needed to bring her long term goal into the present. This is what you must do.

# Plan for the Future, But Work in the Present!

Use the following goal-setting exercises to help you take the first important step in becoming a champion: START WITH THE END IN MIND. Refer to the Goal Setting Guide at the end of this section to help you develop effective goals.

## Goal Exercise #1

1) Write out a list of **ALL** the goals you wish to attain in soccer.

2) Prioritize them in order of importance and in relation to time. That is, label which are short term (up to 30 days), intermediate (4 - 6 months) and long term (a year and up). Remember, intermediate and short term goals should lead you directly to your long term goal.

3) Break the short term goals into smaller chunks (remember the elephant) by developing 2 to 4 mini goals or steps that you can take to help you reach these short term goals. Mini goals should be workable on a daily basis, in practice, or on your own.

4) **ASK THE EXPERTS!** Consult with your coach, sport psychologist, strength trainer, nutritionist, or other experts to help you identify exactly what you need to work on.

5) Check your goals against the Goal Setting Guidelines at the end of this section to be sure that your goals meet all the criteria.

## Guidelines for Successful Goal Setting

1) Make sure the goals are **YOURS** (not your coach's, parents' or friends').

2) Make your goals **CHALLENGING** but **REALISTIC**.

3) Make your goals **SPECIFIC**. Vague and general goals like "I want to be faster or stronger" are not as helpful as "I want to run the 100 in 10.5 seconds" or I want to bench press 200 lbs".

4) Make your goals **MEASURABLE**. You have to be able to specifically monitor your progress.

5) Make your goals **COMPATIBLE**. A goal of wanting to build your speed and endurance is not compatible with a goal of doing extra wind sprints once a month

6) Your goals should be **FLEXIBLE** to allow for **CHANGES**. If you set a goal too high or low, you need to be able to make the appropriate adjustment. Remember, your goals should **NOT** be etched in stone, they should serve as general guidelines for your efforts.

7) Set a **TIME FRAME** or **TARGET** date for each goal. This time frame pressure will help you stay motivated towards completion.

8) Put your goals in **WRITING**. Write down your goals, sign them and keep them continually in front of you. This will help you make more of a commitment to working on them.

9) **PRIORITIZE** your goals. Arrange your goals in relation to their importance to you and your long term objective.

# STEP #2 • The Ultimate Secret to Athletic Success

There is one factor that separates successful athletes from everyone else. It has nothing to do with more talent, ability or God given gifts. It is a factor that can neutralize disabilities and enable a less talented performer to beat a more talented one. It is a simple "secret", so obvious that it is regularly dismissed by most players. It is a four letter word: **WORK**!

The secret to success in soccer is **HARD WORK**. There is no shortcut to excellence. You have to do it the old fashioned way! Athletes who make it in every sport are not necessarily more talented, stronger, or faster. Their edge lies in their work ethic. They **WANT** that goal more and are willing to do all the sweaty, uncomfortable extras that most other athletes will not do.

Your **DESIRE** and attitude will take you much further than your natural talent and skills. Hard work will put success in a picture where no one else can see it. Ask Rocky Blier, Pro Football great and Hall of Famer for the Pittsburgh Steelers. In the late 60's Blier was drafted by the Steelers out of college but never got to play because he was also drafted by Uncle Sam and sent over to Vietnam. During his tour of duty he stepped on a land mine and took shrapnel in his foot and leg. After a military discharge he hobbled back to the States, unable to walk without a limp and excruciating pain.

However, when Blier returned he had this crazy notion that he wanted to pick up his football career where he left off! No one in Pro Football wanted to have anything to do with someone who could barely walk, never mind run. Blier, however, had other things in mind and spent month after painful month **WORKING** to get back in playing shape. He gutted his way through the impossible and not only made the Steeler team, but became All-Pro and was the major reason that the Steelers achieved so much success in the late 60's and early 70's! Was Blier more talented than many of the other players he beat out at his position? **NO**...he was crippled. His secret? He wanted it more and was willing to **WORK, WORK, WORK**.

Not everyone has the physical talent and ability to make the World Cup team. However, if you have a big enough "**WHY**", **AND** you are willing to "pay your dues", then what you accomplish will take you **FAR BEYOND** the normal limitations of your physical abilities!

## If You Want to Become a Champion, It's Up To You

**If you want to go as far as possible in soccer YOU have to take responsibility for your training. NO ONE can make you great except YOU! Too many soccer players put this important responsibility on coaches, parents and everyone else but themselves. When something goes wrong they begin pointing the finger and blaming others, "It was the referee's fault we lost today", "I would have made the team if it wasn't for"..., "I would be a much better player if I had a better coach!"**

This mentality of "**GOOD GAME, GOOD PLAYER, BAD GAME, BAD COACH**" is the way losers think! It is up to **YOU** to take your training seriously and work hard towards **YOUR** goals. When you blow off practice, dog it when the coach is not looking, or complain about having to do extra hard practices and wind sprints, you are only fooling and hurting **YOURSELF**! Remember the 10 most important 2 letter words!

**"IF IT IS TO BE, IT IS UP TO ME!"**

## Step #3 • Champions Believe in Themselves N.M.W. (No Matter What)

**SOCCER PLAYERS ARE LIMITED MOST BY WHAT THEY BELIEVE IS POSSIBLE**. Your belief system can make or break your competitive career on and off the pitch. What you believe can empower you to spectacular play or drag your game right into a poor performance. The one characteristic of successful players is that they have a strong belief in themselves. Even if they suffer setbacks or big failures they maintain a positive belief in themselves and their abilities.

Remember, performance is self-fulfilling. **YOU GET WHAT YOU EXPECT**. It is your belief system that sets this all in motion.

If you do not believe you can do something, you will be less determined and persistent in your efforts to accomplish that task. When you run into setbacks and obstacles, (which you must in order to be successful), you will be less likely to hang in there to see them through. **WHEN YOU FAIL TO PERSIST, YOU WILL PERSIST IN FAILING**! Each time you fail you will have more "evidence" or proof to support your belief that you **CAN NOT** succeed. Thus, you have set in motion the self-fulfilling cycle of losing!

However, if you go into any situation and believe that you **CAN DO** it, a whole different cycle is set into motion. When you fail or run into obstacles, you will keep your determination and persist until you are successful because deep down you know that you can do it. **WHEN YOU PERSIST IN BEING PERSISTENT, YOU HAVE NO CHOICE BUT TO ULTIMATELY REACH THAT GOAL**. This is the self-fulfilling cycle of winning because each success reinforces your "**CAN DO**" beliefs!

If there is one player who always manages to beat you, who plays with you on the pitch like you are a toy, it would be easy for you to stop believing in yourself. However, if you went into your next game against this player and believed that he would again totally embarrass you, your resultant lack of effort would insure that he would turn your face red **AGAIN**!

To become a champion, you must start by learning to believe in yourself. You can learn to develop the belief of champions. **THE BIRTH OF EXCELLENCE BEGINS WITH THE UNDERSTANDING THAT YOU CAN CHOOSE YOUR BELIEFS**. You can choose beliefs that empower you or those that hold you back! It is just like having your own garden. What you reap in terms of performance depends on what you sow, or your beliefs.

## "YOUR MIND IS LIKE A GARDEN. WHAT YOU HARVEST DEPENDS ON WHAT YOU PLANT. PLANT WHEAT AND IT WILL GROW. PLANT STINKWEED AND THAT IS WHAT YOU WILL GET."

Recently I spoke to a freshman wrestler on the phone who had just upset the defending State Champion. The funny thing about his victory was that he did not know **WHO** his opponent was. **NO ONE ON THE TEAM HAD TOLD HIM HE WAS SUPPOSED TO LOSE**. This young man did **NOT** know how great his opponent was and so did **NOT** develop any negative beliefs about the outcome of his match, beliefs which would have surely held him back.

Your beliefs are so powerful that they can neutralize a handicap that exists or create one that is not there. If you follow baseball, you probably know all about Jim Abbott. In High School Jim was a pitching Phenom who averaged 2 strikeouts an inning in his senior year and batted .458. He turned down a Major League contract to go to the University of Michigan, and in 1988 he pitched the USA team to an Olympic Gold. Now he is pitching for the Anaheim Angels and is considered to be one of the better pitchers in the Big Leagues.

If you know about Jim Abbott, then you know he was born with only one hand! His right arm stops at his wrist. As a pitcher, he is so good that opposing batters do not know he is handicapped! This is because Abbott does not know he is handicapped and consequently he never ACTED handicapped . He grew up believing what his parents had continually told him:

**"THERE IS NOTHING YOU CAN NOT ACCOMPLISH IN THIS WORLD. YOU HAVE NO HANDICAPS. YOU HAVE NO LIMITATIONS. PERHAPS YOU MAY HAVE TO FIND YOUR OWN UNIQUE WAY OF DOING THINGS. IT MAY TAKE YOU LONGER THAN EVERYONE ELSE. YOU MAY HAVE TO WORK TWICE AS HARD AS EVERYONE ELSE. BUT YOU HAVE NO LIMITS."**

Too many athletes are far more limited than Jim Abbott. They are **NOT** limited physically. It is far more tragic than that! They are limited mentally by what they **BELIEVE** is possible for them. As a player and a person, you have tremendous potential. **YOU HAVE A SUPER ATHLETE INSIDE. BUT**, you must start to believe in that super athlete in order to get him or her out!

# A FABLE ABOUT BELIEFS AND LIMITS

Once upon a time, a farmer noticed some unusual activity behind his barn which continued for several weeks. Two huge majestic birds continually circled the area, coming and going at different times. When the farmer went to investigate, he noticed a huge nest perched at the top of the barn. After a little research he realized that the birds were eagles.

One day he decided to try a little experiment. He snuck up to the nest, took one of the eggs and placed it in one of the chicken coops with some other eggs in a hen's nest. Two weeks passed and all the eggs in the chicken's nest hatched, including the strange looking, larger one. All the newborn chicks were then taken out by their mother to parade around the barnyard and to learn all the things that chicks need to know, i.e. how to walk like a chick, scratch for feed, peck for corn, etc. All the chicks learned their lessons well, including the huge, funny looking one that had come from that strange egg.

Months passed and the chicks grew into chickens. While they would flap their wings and squawk a lot, they never flew because everyone knows that chickens can not fly. The biggest "chicken", which looked very much like an eagle, followed all the other chickens around, acting like a chicken, which is of course what he believed himself to be.

One day he was out in the middle of the barnyard scratching for feed when this majestic bird soared overhead. Everyone in the yard stopped to gawk. The big "chicken", who was really an eagle, asked King Rooster, the wise old sage of the barn yard, what kind of bird could fly so powerfully and gracefully. King Rooster proudly replied, "That my son is an Eagle, the greatest bird of all" The funny looking chicken gazed wistfully up to the clouds and replied, "Oh how I wish I were an eagle so that I might fly like that." Whereupon King Rooster and everyone else listening began to laugh. "Do not be silly, son", the rooster advised, "You are a chicken and everyone knows that chickens **CAN'T** fly!"

And so for the rest of his life, the big, funny looking chicken stayed in the barn yard acting like a chicken and never flew.

## "Belief in Limits Creates Limited People"

Is it easy for you to learn to believe in yourself? Like everything else I have been discussing, it takes hard work and consistent practice. However, this will be harder than most things you have to do because it involves other people.

Too many athletes today are not into taking risks and going for it. These athletes are more concerned about fitting in than pursuing their own dreams. If you have a big goal in soccer, a huge dream, then the one thing you will not be able to do is "fit in." If you decide to really **GO FOR IT**, you will set yourself apart from the majority of people your age who are heavily into being average.

People who have big goals and channel their energies to work on achieving those goals usually become open targets for ridicule.

They are made fun of and put down for thinking they can achieve **THAT**! It is the High School freshman who spoke to me after one of my talks who had a dream of going to the Atlanta Olympics in 1996. His "friends" and acquaintances thought that was the most ridiculous thing they had ever heard. It is the 6th grader who wants to play in the 1998 World Cup and gets laughed at for having great aspirations.

It is very easy to be mediocre and average. It takes no particular energy or strength to fit in with the gang. But if being average and being liked is one of your priorities, you will never become a winner! You have to dare to be different! You have to **BELIEVE** in your dream and have the **GUTS** to openly pursue it. When Cassius Clay was growing up he told everyone who would listen that someday he was going to be the heavyweight champion of the world! People in his home town thought this was one of the craziest things they ever heard! As Mohammed Ali, Clay reached his goal and became one of the greatest boxers ever!

Now you do not have to do what Ali did and tell the world that you are the greatest. The **ONLY** person you have to convince is **YOURSELF**! This will not be easy when people all around you are telling you it can not be done. Some of these people really care about you and do not want to see you hurt or disappointed. Many others are simply uncomfortable with the fact that they are not going for it in their lives. When they see someone else really striving for excellence, they feel inadequate. If you are pursuing your dream, you remind them that they are not. Their answer? They "rain on your parade" so-to-speak.

# FIVE STEPS TO LEARNING TO BELIEVE IN YOURSELF

**#1 DO NOT LISTEN TO THE EXPERTS.** Do not listen to anyone who tells you that you can not reach your goal. The **ONLY** experts you should listen to are those who support your dream, encourage you and provide you with strategies for getting there. In 1954 the "experts" tried to tell Roger Bannister that the human body could not run a mile in under 4 minutes. In the 60's they tried to tell us that we could never put a human on the moon. There were and still are many "experts" who claim that US Soccer can never be a dominant power in the game. For every dream, there are hundreds of 'experts' waiting in the wings to explain why that dream **CAN NOT** be realized.

**#2 ELIMINATE WORDS LIKE "CAN'T", "NEVER" AND "IMPOS-SIBLE".** These words are self-limiting. Rip them out of the dictionary in your mind. When you use them on yourself you will hold yourself back. You do **NOT** really know what is possible in your life. Make a conscious effort on a daily basis to rid yourself of this kind of self-limiting language. If you are going to use words like "can't", add "**YET**" to them. "I can not do that **YET**" means that up until now you have not been able to, **BUT, IT IS** still possible in the future. Remember, the language you use on yourself directly effects your performance and whether or not you will achieve your goals.

**#3 PRACTICE DOING THE IMPOSSIBLE ON A DAILY BASIS.** There are two kinds of impossibles: Impossible impossibles and possible impossibles. The impossible impossibles are things like flying, running faster than a speeding bullet, stopping a tractor trailer going 90 mph., etc. These things you can not practice without serious risk to your life. However, you **CAN** practice the possible impossibles. These are things that you **THINK** or **KNOW** that you can not do. On a daily basis you want to begin to challenge those limiting beliefs and move towards these tasks. Maybe you do not think you can juggle non-stop for 5 minutes, run a sub-5 minute mile, develop a real powerful kick, stay calm under pressure or talk in front of a group. Take one thing you think you can not do, and work on it every day. It does not even have to have anything to do with soccer. **EVERY TIME YOU CHALLENGE YOUR LIMITING BELIEFS BY MOVING TOWARDS THEM, YOU WILL EXPAND THEM!**

**#4 SURROUND YOURSELF WITH "GO-FOR-IT" PEOPLE.** Make sure you have people around you who totally support your dream and goal. If your friends belittle you, think seriously about getting new ones. Reaching a big goal is hard enough without having people around you throwing up obstacles.

**#5 TALK TO, READ ABOUT, WATCH AND LISTEN TO PEOPLE WHO HAVE OVERCOME OBSTACLES TO MAKE IT.** You can expand your belief system by reading about or talking to other people who have done the "impossible." They will provide you with real life examples that anything is possible. If you immerse yourself in books, audio-tapes and videos of these kinds of people, it will help you firm up your beliefs that **YOU CAN DO IT** too!

# Step #4 • Champions Take Risks – The GOYA Factor

The major difference between positive thinking and positive believing is **ACTION**. People who **REALLY** believe in themselves backup that belief with action. If you want to become a champion you have to take risks. That is what being a peak performer on the pitch is all about. You can **NEVER** have a great game if you play it safe or cautious! You have to be willing to 'go out on a limb' if you want to be able to taste the fruits of success and victory.

Too many athletes spend too much time thinking and talking about what they will do. Not enough of their energy is focused on action. Talent, ability, and the best strategies in the world will **NOT** help you if you never use them.

A few years ago I worked with a very talented player who had the physical potential to play soccer on a national level. He had a great coach who exposed him to all the physical and technical strategies he needed to make it. He came to work with me in order to develop mental toughness. I taught him everything I know about the mental side of the game and provided him with the skills that would help him compete successfully at the top. Between his coach and me we had all the bases covered. All except one! **HIM!** He never practiced or seriously worked on any of the skills we taught him. He talked about his training a lot, how good he was going to get, and how far he would go, **BUT** he never took serious **ACTION**.

He is a classic example of the athlete with "permanent potential." Because he failed to **GOYA (GET OFF YOUR BACKSIDE)**, he never went anywhere. You must be willing to put yourself and your skills on the line. You must be willing to take risks! It is your actions that will motivate you!

**"DO NOT WAIT TO GET MOTIVATED BEFORE YOU TAKE ACTION, TAKE ACTION AND THEN YOU WILL GET MOTIVATED"**

# Step #5 • Champions Use Their Failures as Stepping Stones to Success

Do you want to know **THE** most important secret to reaching your dreams? The one strategy in soccer and life that will guarantee you success? The mental attitude that separates the winners from losers inside and outside of sports? The answers to all three have to do with **FAILURE**, and how you respond to it.

I mentioned that winners regularly take risks. They put themselves on the line. They go for it! One of the very **COMMON** things that will happen to you when you do this is called **FAILURE**. While you may have been told that you have to go out on a limb to get the fruit, you may not know that frequently when you are in that precarious position, you will fall.

Failure and setbacks are part of the scenery you pass on the road to success. You can not reach your goals unless you can get beyond them. Winners know this well. In fact, one of the characteristics of successful athletes is the ability to deal with failure.

Because they are willing to take more risks, champions actually fail **MORE** than most other athletes. However, it is their attitude towards their failures that enables them to get back on their feet and rise to great heights. Champions view their failures as **OPPORTUNITIES** to learn and improve as athletes. They do not **LIKE** losing or failing. I have never met a champion who did. However, when they do fail or suffer some other setback they use it as feedback to get stronger. You have two options available to you when you fail:

1)  You can mistakenly view the failure as evidence of your inadequacies and shortcomings. In this way you can emotionally use the failure to bring yourself down.

2)  You can learn from the failure by using it as feedback, as a way to improve and become a smarter, stronger player.

If you take option #1 after your failures, you will be left feeling depressed, worthless and unmotivated. Setbacks and failures will be devastating and hang you up for long periods of time. Further, you will be more likely to quit a quest long before you reach your goals.

If you go for option #2, you will rebound very quickly from your setbacks. Failure will not adversely effect your self-esteem, but instead will leave you even more determined and motivated to reach your goal.

Option #2 is the **ONLY** option for winners. You must view your setbacks as **TEMPORARY** and opportunities to learn. When Kareem Abdul Jabbar played at UCLA as Lew Alcindor, the NCAA banned his best shot, the dunk! The NCAA felt that it was not fair for someone to have Alcindor's size advantage. This setback could have left Alcindor a weaker, embittered player. Instead, he viewed it as an opportunity to develop a more deadly offensive weapon, the "skyhook."

Every setback or failure has two sides. You can view it as a positive or a negative, It is your **CHOICE**! You can control your attitude. This is even the case with injuries. Very often an injury will temporarily take away your favorite weapon or strategy and force you to strengthen other parts of your game. In the long run this can only make you a better all around player.

Understand that a baby can **ONLY** learn to walk by falling! With each fall the baby's muscle memory is provided with valuable feedback to learn how to stand, balance and move. Without the repeated failures there could be no walking. That is why I always say that **ANYTHING WORTH DOING IS WORTH DOING BADLY** (at first)! Remember, there is really only one way you can fail. Try something once or twice and then give up!

**IT IS ABSOLUTELY CRITICAL** that you change your attitude to failing, setbacks and losses. If you go out on the pitch and are afraid of making mistakes, getting hurt, or losing, you will physically tighten yourself up and play poorly. You play your very best soccer when you have nothing to lose and when you are **NOT THINKING ABOUT THE OUTCOME**. Losing is part of sports and not something to worry about. If you make a game so important that the thought of losing freaks you out, you will **NOT** play well in that match!

Recently, I worked with a very talented collegiate keeper who was trying to make a comeback from a season ending rib injury. She had come out aggressively on a cross ball, lunged to catch the ball and, while fully extended, she caught an opponent's knee in her ribs, breaking three of them. The next season she was back in goal, but very tentative. Even though her injury had completely healed, she played as if it might happen again at any moment. Her aggressive, challenging style of play which had made her so dominant as a keeper was gone. Instead of focusing on the ball, developing play and what she needed to do, she was suddenly preoccupied with getting caught in that vulnerable extended position again. She dreaded cross balls and refused to come out of the net to play them. It is this kind of attitude concerning injuries, mistakes and failures that will almost certainly insure that they continue to happen.

Your focus must be on the game and what you **WANT** to happen. **NOT** on what you are afraid will happen. Learn from your failures and let them go. Treat them as a **PASSING** thing. **DO NOT TALK ABOUT FAILURES USING "PERMANENT" LANGUAGE.**

"This **ALWAYS** happens to me." "I am just a head case." "I can **NEVER** play well under pressure." "I **CAN'T** play that position."

"Permanent" language will make your failures seem insurmountable, an inescapable **PART** of you and with you for life. Remember, **FAILURE IS MERELY DELAYED SUCCESS** as long as you view it in temporary and specific terms:

"Whew, I got beaten badly **TODAY**. But next game I will know how to play her so that does not happen again." "I blew that scoring opportunity because I got too nervous. Coach told me there are some techniques that he can teach me to better handle those pressured situations." "I missed that penalty kick because I was thinking too much about what the keeper was going to do. Next time I will stick to my own routine."

If you refer to your setbacks and failures using this kind of **TEMPORARY** and **SPECIFIC** language, you will be left feeling positive and optimistic. This is

the only constructive attitude to have when you are dealing with adversity.
**FAILURE IS FEEDBACK AND FEEDBACK IS THE BREAKFAST OF CHAMPIONS**

# Chapter 3
## Handling the Pressure of Competition

The foundation of mental toughness is your ability to stay calm and composed under pressure. If you can not control your level of pre-game and during game nervousness your play will **ALWAYS** be erratic and you will never reach your potential as a player. All the talent, speed and ball handling skills in the world will not help you if you get too uptight before you play. Excessive nervousness will neutralize your edge and leave you physically tight and mentally tentative. This section is designed to teach you **HOW** to read your own level of nervousness and **WHAT** to do if you find yourself getting too uptight before or during a big game.

## The Causes of Stress

There are many factors that can cause you to become too uptight and not allow you to play your best. The importance of the match, size of the crowd, strength of your opponents, weather and field conditions, etc., etc., etc. You may **THINK** these are the reasons that you start to feel nervous, that these elements are **CAUSING** your stress. This, however is **NOT** the case in relation to stress:

**IT IS NOT WHAT IS HAPPENING TO YOU OR AROUND YOU THAT IS IMPORTANT, BUT WHAT IS HAPPENING INSIDE YOU THAT COUNTS.**

Opponents, officials, field or weather conditions **DO NOT** make you tense. Instead, it is what you **SAY TO YOURSELF** about the opponents, officials or playing conditions that is the **REAL** culprit in raising your anxiety level to the ceiling. The commentary of your "inner coach" is what really causes your stress reaction. How else can you explain the fact that two very good shooters setting up to hit game deciding penalty kicks often have much different results. One shooter, regardless of how big the game is, consistently scores, while the other shooter frequently blows this scoring opportunity. Both shooters face the same stressors. The difference is **HOW** they interpret those stressors, and deal with them!

To put it very simply. **PEOPLE, PLACES AND SITUATIONS DO NOT MAKE YOU UPTIGHT, YOU MAKE YOURSELF UPTIGHT**! The **BIGGEST** cause of choking is trying to control the uncontrollable. The uncontrollables in a match are all the things that are **TOTALLY** out of your control: The weather, conditions of the pitch, officiating, crowd, winning and losing, the play of your opponents, your coach etc.

If you choose to focus on, or try to "control" these uncontrollables you will make yourself too uptight to play good ball. This means that if someone in the stands is razzing you and you start to get upset, you are focusing on, and trying to control, an uncontrollable. Likewise, if the conditions of the field or officiating are less than optimal and you are wasting energy thinking about them, you are trying to control an uncontrollable. If you let a goal score against your team and you keep thinking about how you blew it, you are focusing on the **PAST**, a **HUGE** uncontrollable.

Mentally tough soccer players focus on the one thing that they can **ALWAYS** control in a game, themselves. **YOU** are in **TOTAL** control of how **YOU CHOOSE** to react to all of the uncontrollables in a match. Nothing or nobody can stress you out unless you allow it to happen!

## Understand the Relationship Between Stress and Performance

The graph in figure #1 shows the relationship between stress and performance. It depicts how well you play at different levels of physiological arousal or nervousness. If you want to become a mentally tough player it is your job to develop a **WORKING** understanding of this graph. Let me show you how:

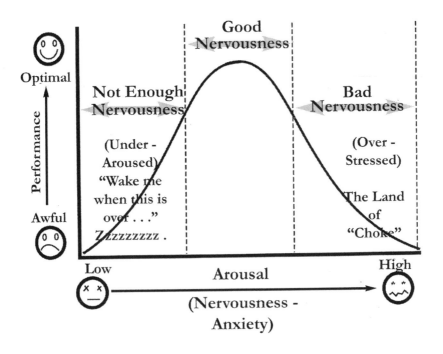

The **VERTICAL AXIS** measures how well you are performing. If you are low on the graph you are "giving an awful performance". If you are high on the graph you are "walking on water" and having a peak performance. The **HORIZONTAL AXIS** measures how nervous or stressed out you are. If you are way over on the left side of the graph you are not nervous at all, you are basically asleep. As you move further and further to the right your anxiety level progressively increases. If you are on the right side of the graph you are having a full blown anxiety attack!

The graph shows that as you get nervous pre-game, your level of performance improves. If you continue to add stress, your performance reaches a peak. If you continue to add stress, your play begins to disintegrate and your performance declines.

On the graph I have marked off 3 kinds of nervousness: Good, Bad, and Not Enough. It is important for you to understand that **EVERY SOCCER PLAYER FEELS NERVOUS BEFORE A BIG GAME**. Some nervousness is important for you to get mentally and physically prepared to play your best. However, you have to make sure that you are at the "right" amount of nervousness for you. If you are "not enough" nervous your play will be flat and uninspired. If you are into "bad" nervousness you will be physically too tight to play well. You have to be into "good" nervousness in order to play your very best. How can you tell the difference?

# Reading Your Own Nervousness

Every player on the team has the performance arousal curve working for him. However, every athlete is different. Everyone responds differently to pressure. What stresses one player into "bad" nervousness gets a second player into "good" nervousness and does not get a third athlete out of "not enough" nervousness. It is therefore critical for you as an athlete to be able to "read" your own levels of nervousness and to be able to clearly tell the difference between all three. As a coach, you must be able to do this with each of the athletes on your squad. If, for example, you know that you are into "bad" nervousness before the game or that all important penalty kick, then you can do something constructive to calm yourself down before your performance suffers. Awareness is the key.

There are three ways you experience anxiety or nervousness, and therefore three ways you can read your level of pre-game or pre-performance nervousness:

1) Physiologically - physical changes in your body
2) Mentally - changes in your thoughts and self-talk
3) Behaviorally - changes in how you act

As you begin to get nervous, your body immediately responds **PHYSICALLY** with increased heart and pulse rate, faster and shallower breathing, tighter muscles, butterflies in your stomach and/or feelings of nausea, cold hands and feet, dry mouth, increased sweating, frequent yawning and an urge to urinate.

**MENTALLY**, your thoughts have a tendency to speed up, you experience difficulty concentrating, you tend to become critical of yourself and others, you begin to entertain self-doubts, and you find yourself locking your concentration in on the source of your anxiety.

As you get nervous your **BEHAVIORS** change. You may stop moving and sit quietly, you may start jumping around and talking non-stop. You may get very serious or very giddy. You may become hostile or angry, or you may engage in nervous habits or superstitious rituals.

All of these changes are neither good nor bad. They are simply indicators of what happens to you when you get nervous. Your job is to figure out which of these changes are associated with "good" nervousness, "bad" nervousness and "not enough" nervousness. That way you will be in a position to change your arousal level if necessary.

# READING NERVOUSNESS
## Exercise #1 Discovering "Good Nervousness"

The purpose of this first exercise is to help you get to know the pre-performance signs of good nervousness, that is, what happens physically, mentally and behaviorally when you are in a state of "good" nervousness. By recognizing what thoughts, feelings and behaviors lead you to great games, you can more easily identify the pre-performance state you need to achieve to produce your best efforts.

Sit comfortably in a quiet place where you will be undisturbed for a period of 5-15 minutes. Have a paper and pencil handy. Think back to the last time you had a great game, when you were really pleased with your performance. Close your eyes and mentally take yourself back to this game, just before it began. See, hear and feel in as much detail **NOW**, everything you did back then.

A) Examine the **PHYSICAL** sensations you were feeling just before the game or before the penalty kick. If you had butterflies, where were they in your body? What did your arms and legs feel like? Did you feel sick to your stomach? Did you feel tired or energized? Were you yawning a lot? How about your breathing? Take a few minutes to jot down all of the physical sensations of "good" nervousness.

B) Next, examine what was going on **MENTALLY** before the game. What was the dialogue of your inner coach? What kind of self-talk were you aware of? What were you focused on? Did you entertain self-doubts? Were you anticipating the start of the match? Now write down what you can remember to be these mental signs of "good" nervousness.

C) Finally, how did you **BEHAVE** before the game? Did you sit quietly or jump around? Did you listen to a walkman, joke with friends or talk about the match? What kind of rituals or nervous behaviors did you engage in? Write down all the behavioral signs of "good" nervousness.

D) Repeat A-C examining several other great games that you have played.

# Exercise #2 Discovering "Bad" Nervousness

Like the above exercise, the purpose of this one is to help you develop an awareness of your pre-game level of arousal. However, this exercise will specifically help you recognize the physical, mental and behavioral signs of "bad" nervousness. Knowing that you are slipping into "bad" nervousness will allow you to utilize one or more tension control techniques to bring you back to "good" nervousness and optimal play.

Sit comfortably in a quiet place where you will be undisturbed for 5-15 minutes. Like the first exercise, have a pencil and paper nearby. Think back to the last time you had a particularly **AWFUL** game, a time when you felt totally frustrated and disappointed in your play. A time when your poor play was directly related to being **TOO** nervous. Close your eyes and mentally return to this time. See, hear, and feel, in as much detail as possible, all that went on at that time.

A) Examine the **PHYSICAL** sensations that were associated with "bad" nervousness. What did you feel in your arms or legs? Were you overly tired? Did you feel sick to your stomach? Butterflies? If so, where? Write down all the physical signs of "bad" nervousness.

B) What was going on **MENTALLY** before this game or specific situation? What were you telling yourself? What were you focusing on? If your mind was racing, what was it racing over? What expectations did you have that day? Were you dreading the match or hoping it would be over? Write down all the mental signs of "bad" nervousness.

C) How did you **ACT** pre-game or pre-kick? Did you hang out with teammates or stay to yourself? Were you joking around or acting angry? Were you moving pre-game, if so how? Jot down all the behavioral signs of "bad" nervousness.

D) Repeat A-C examining several other games in which you choked or played poorly because of your nerves.

**NOTE:** If you are the kind of athlete who plays poorly because you are under aroused or into "not enough" nervousness, repeat this exercise using steps A-D examining games in which you played poorly because of this.

# Exercise #3 • Compare and Contrast

Take a few minutes now just to review the differences you have discovered between "good", "bad", and (if appropriate) "not enough" nervousness. If you examined several games in each category you should begin to see a pattern developing. "Bad" nervousness looks, feels and sounds differently than "good" nervousness. In the beginning the differences may seem slight or very subtle. If you are patient and look carefully at your games in this way, soon you will be able to quickly recognize the thoughts, physical sensations and behaviors that represent all three kinds of pre-performance nervousness.

## Coping with "Bad" Nervousness

If you are too nervous before a game or a crucial penalty kick you will not perform to your potential. If you know that you are into "bad" nervousness, what is needed are some ways to calm yourself down so that you can get back in control. This section will present a number of relaxation strategies that, **IF PRACTICED**, will help you turn "bad" nervousness into "good" nervousness.

## Coping Strategy #1 • Act As If You Are "Good" Nervous

One of the first things you can do to help stay calm under stress is try to repeat all the signs of "good" nervousness before you play. For example, if before your best games you went off by yourself, focused on your task for the match, and mentally rehearsed the game, then you should do this before every game. However, if sitting by yourself and concentrating on the game causes you to get too uptight, (and you know that bouncing off the walls, joking around with teammates and having non-game related thoughts causes you to play well), then make sure you are hanging around with teammates and **NOT** discussing the game before it starts. Even if you are uptight before a game, try repeating the self-talk and behaviors that accompany "good" nervousness.

## Coping Strategy #2 • Simulation

The **BEST** way to learn how to handle competitive pressures on a daily basis is in **PRACTICE**. If you are accustomed to practicing under stress, you will play well under pressure. This is the concept of **STATE BOUND LEARNING**. If you understand this concept it will help you excel when the heat of competition is turned up high.

State bound learning is easily explained by the following experiment: Psychologists took rats and put them in an inebriated state, i.e. they got them drunk. Once in this state the rats were taught to run a maze. As long as the rats were in this drunken state, they knew the maze well. However, once the rats became sober, a different state, they could no- longer figure the maze out. Once back in the drunken state they were again able to remember their teachings and run the maze.

Most athletes practice in a different mental and emotional state than exists during a game. In practice they are relaxed and rarely pressured. However, big match situations present an entirely different mental and emotional state. The best coaches and athletes in this sport intuitively understand the concept of state bound learning. They make sure that their practices simulate as closely as possible the physical and mental stressors that are presented in games.

Anson Dorrance, coach of the University of North Carolina's women's program and former US Women's Team coach makes his college team practices even more stressful than games. His players are trained on a daily basis to deal with pressure. Since soccer is a series of individual duels, Coach Dorrance recreates these battles for his players in their conditioning and training sessions.

Anson understands that **FAMILIARITY BINDS ANXIETY**. That is, anything you have to confront day after day will ultimately become so familiar that it will no longer cause you stress. It is the **UNEXPECTED** that will knock you off center and cause you to freak out. By integrating competitive elements into your practice sessions, by trying to simulate game pressures as much as possible, you will best train yourself to handle the heat of competition.

This is the concept of **ETU.** i.e. **EXPECT THE UNEXPECTED**. If you can anticipate the kinds of things that would normally psyche you out, then practice (mentally and physically) successfully handling them, you will not get knocked off center when they occur. If you play keeper, and a rowdy crowd has a tendency to get to you, practice with a crowd razzing you. If you have a tendency to stress out when you are beaten or make mistakes, practice rebounding quickly whenever these situations occur in practice. Maybe you can even have the coach arrange for some of the "crowd" watching your practice sessions to really get on your case every time you mess up.

There are no limits to how much you can use simulation to help you prepare for any pressured situation when the simulation is **MENTAL**. Many soccer players will pretend that various drills or scrimmages in practice are important points in a game, or they will take the simulation home with them and imagine the game situations over and over again. They will "experience" themselves confronting any stressor and successfully handling it.

Simulation is all about perfect practice. **IT IS PERFECT PRACTICE, OR PRACTICE THAT BEST PREPARES YOU FOR COMPETITION, THAT MAKES PERFECT**. For example, while it is important for you to physically practice the technique involved in penalty kicks over and over again, you will get far more out of these practice sessions if you can create more game-like situations for yourself. Taking each kick as if a game was on the line, going through a set pre-kick routine, having a "Crowd" on hand, etc. will help you get much more out of penalty kick practice than just standing there and cranking off rapid fire kicks.

# Coping Strategy #3 • Progressive Muscle Relaxation (PMR)

Previously, I mentioned that relaxation is a foundation skill in mental toughness training. It helps you handle the pressure of competition, cools your body down in between and after big games, enables you to maintain the right focus of concentration and properly prepares you for the use of mental rehearsal. Without the ability to relax, you can never reach your potential as a player.

**PROGRESSIVE MUSCLE RELAXATION** is a foundation skill in relaxation training. It teaches you not only **HOW** to relax, but also how to **RECOGNIZE** exactly where you put tension in your body. It is an easy skill to teach as a coach and, with practice, an easy skill to learn. Like any of the relaxation skills that follow, mastery comes from regular practice.

Coaches should plan on spending 20-25 minutes of two practices in the **BEGINNING** of the season, teaching players this skill in a group setting. Athletes should then take it upon themselves to practice PMR at night before bedtime for approximately two weeks. After this period of time you will be able to streamline the exercise and relax very quickly.

In PMR, you work your way through the muscle groupings of your body alternating contraction with relaxation. You should hold the tension in each muscle group for 10 seconds and be sure that contraction is no more than 90% of your strength. Remember to maintain relaxation in all other muscles except the ones being tightened.

**PREPARATION:** Allow 20-25 minutes for each PMR session in an environment that is free from distractions. You may want to take the following directions and make your own relaxation tape. Slowly read them into a tape recorder, allowing 10 seconds for each contraction and 10 seconds for each release. You can even dub in relaxing music in the background. Lie comfortably on your back, feet spread about 18 inches apart, hands by your sides, palms up. Close your eyes.

## Procedure:

1. Begin to tighten all the muscles up and down your right leg until you reach 90% tension. Pointing the toes either toward or away from your head will help you increase tension. Raising the leg one half inch off the ground also helps to tighten muscles. Hold the leg tension for 10 seconds Study the tension. Feel it.

2. Repeat to yourself, "Let go" as you allow the leg to relax, letting the tension flow out onto the floor. Feel the difference in your leg now, inhale slowly and deeply, filling your abdomen, pause, and then exhale.

3. Repeat the entire procedure for your right leg again, noting the difference

between being tight in that area and loose. End by inhaling deeply and exhaling.

4. Tighten all the muscles up and down your left leg and hold the tensionfor 10 seconds. Study the tension as you hold it. Repeat to yourself, "Let go" and let the tension slowly drain from the left leg. Note the sensations that accompany relaxation...the heaviness, warmth, tingling, lightness or other feelings that are associated with looseness. Inhale, pause, and exhale.

5. Repeat the entire procedure for your left leg again, then inhale, pause, and exhale.

6. Tighten your buttocks muscles to 90% tension and hold it. Become aware of the feelings. Repeat the "Let go". After 10 seconds let the tension drain from this area. Feel the looseness. Inhale, pause, exhale.

7. Repeat procedure for the buttocks muscles. Inhale...exhale.

8. Tighten abdominal muscles noting the sensations of tension here. Hold it, then "Let go" and allow the tension to flow from this area. Feel the difference. Study it closely. Inhale, then exhale.

9. Repeat procedure for the abdominal muscles. Inhale, exhale.

10. Tighten all the muscles of the chest and those across the back of the shoulders by pushing your shoulder blades back and into the floor. Feel the tension, study it, now "Let go" and feel the relaxation as it flows into this part of your body. Inhale, pause, exhale.

11. Repeat entire procedure for chest and shoulders. Inhale, pause, exhale.

12. Tense the muscles of both arms by slowly making a fist and increasing tension to 90%. Notice the feelings of tension up and down the arms. "Let go" and allow the tension to drain down your arms from your shoulders to your fingertips. Inhale, pause, exhale.

13. Repeat entire procedure for both arms, becoming aware of the sensations that accompany tension and relaxation. Inhale, pause, exhale.

14. Tense the muscles in your neck by pressing down with your head into the surface that you are resting on. Notice the tension in this area. Feel it, then "Let go" and allow the tightness to slowly drain from your neck. Study the difference here. Inhale, pause, exhale.

15. Repeat procedure for the neck. Inhale, pause, exhale.

16. Tighten your jaw muscles by clenching your teeth together. Note the feelings of tightness in this area. Feel it, then "Let go" and allow the tension to drain from your jaws. Inhale, pause, exhale.

17. Repeat entire procedure for your jaw muscles. Inhale, pause, exhale.

18. Tense the muscles in your face, grimace, frown, clench your teeth. Hold the tension and feel what that is like. "Let go" and allow all the facial muscles to relax and soften. Feel the difference. Inhale, pause, exhale.

19. Repeat procedure for your face muscles. Inhale, pause, exhale.

20. Tighten all the muscles in your body to 90% tension. Your arms, legs, buttocks, abdomen, chest, shoulders, neck, face and feel the tension. Hold it for 10 seconds and then "Let go" and slowly allow your body to become totally loose and limp. Inhale, pause, exhale.

21. Repeat procedure for your entire body. Inhale, pause, exhale.

22. If any areas of your body remain tense, focus on them by tightening, holding the tension, then letting go.

Understand that you must first learn the skill of relaxation in a non-stressful environment. Once you have gotten proficient at PMR, you will have the ability to quickly relax anywhere.

# Developing a Relaxation Cue For Transferring Your Skill to the Pitch

Once you have learned any technique to lower your level of stress, you can develop a relaxation CUE. A relaxation cue is a personal symbol or reminder that you can use to help you calm yourself quickly and effectively regardless of the environment. When you are under stress, simply focusing on that cue will be sufficient to help you get back in control.

At the end of your PMR practice (or any other), focus on the feelings of relaxation in your body. While you are feeling these sensations allow yourself to come up with a cue or symbol that you will use to represent these relaxed feelings. Your symbol can be a word, "cool", "calm", "chill", "loose" etc.; a phrase, "Let go", "I am in charge", "I am calm and collected", etc.; a color, light blue, pink, sea green, etc.; an image, a wave, beach, lake, mountain, etc.; or a kinesthetic feeling in your body. Once you have picked out a cue, and **WHILE** you are still relaxed do the following: Inhale and focus on the relaxation. Exhale and focus on your cue. Inhale and feel the relaxation, exhale and repeat that cue to yourself. End **EVERY** relaxation session with 10-12 slow breaths where you focus on your relaxation cue while you feel those relaxed sensations.

# Coping Strategy #4 • Autogenic Training (AT)

Certain physical sensations regularly accompany a relaxed state: heaviness or lightness in arms and legs, a feeling of warmth in the limbs, slower heart beat, slower and more even respiration, and a coolness in the forehead. Because your thoughts have a tremendous influence over your body, it is possible to control how relaxed or tense you are by what you say to yourself. AT is the ability to create a state of physical relaxation on cue. By repeatedly giving yourself suggestions in order, you can, with practice, control your physiological responses, including heart beat, blood pressure, respiration and body temperature, to achieve a relaxed state under big game pressure. In the beginning, you may need to spend 15-20 minutes per session. With practice, like PMR, you will be able to completely relax on command in less than a minute.

# Preparation:

Find a quiet place that is free from distractions. Sit comfortably, back straight, feet flat on the floor, arms uncrossed. You will do each of the five steps in sequence. Have a clock handy to time yourself. Read over the instructions for each step before you do it so that the phrases will be clear in your mind. Close your eyes and try to develop a **PASSIVE, LET-IT HAPPEN** attitude as opposed to a **MAKE-IT-HAPPEN** one. Initially you may not be able to achieve some or all of the desired feelings. This is quite natural and is expected as part of the learning process. **DO NOT** respond by **TRYING HARDER!**

# Procedure:

1.  **HEAVINESS OF THE LIMBS**. Repeat over and over for about 4 minutes, "my hands are beginning to feel very heavy...they are feeling heavier and heavier...my arms are feeling heavier and heavier...my legs and feet are feeling heavier and heavier..I can feel the heaviness moving up and down my arms and legs... heavier and heavier."

2.  **WARMTH IN THE LIMBS**. Repeat over and over again for about 4 minutes, "My hands are beginning to feel warm...they are feeling warmer and warmer...the warmth is spreading up my arms...warmer and warmer...my legs and feet are feeling warmer and warmer."

3. **CARDIAC REGULATION**. Repeat over and over for 4 minutes, "My heart is becoming slower and more regular...it is becoming slower and more consistent...my heart beat is becoming very regular and very slow."

4. **BREATHING REGULATION**. Repeat over and over for 4 minutes, "My breathing is becoming slower and more regular...slower and slower...slow and regular."

5. **COOLNESS IN THE FOREHEAD**. Repeat over and over for 4 minutes, "My forehead is beginning to feel cool...it is feeling cooler and cooler", etc.

# Coping Strategy #5 • Breathing Exercises

One of the first places that stress hits you physiologically is in your breathing. As you begin to experience that stressful situation, your breathing begins to speed up and get shallower. When you are relaxed, your breathing is deep and in your diaphragm. With increasing stress your respiration begins to move upward until, under extreme stress, you have a tendency to either hyperventilate or hold your breath. I have seen many scoring opportunities blown because the player was so uptight that he forgot to breathe as he went to kick. I realize that this may sound silly, but if you have ever "choked", perhaps you can relate to what I am saying. Very shallow breathing kills your endurance, because you do not get enough oxygen to your body, and makes concentration impossible. Further, if you hold your breath as you attempt a penalty kick, your muscles will be much tighter than they would be if you were breathing normally or exhaling on execution.

Probably the **FASTEST** way for you to get yourself or a player back "up the curve" is to change the rate and depth of breathing. By taking slow, diaphragmatic breaths when you are in a tense situation you will be able to calm yourself quickly and effectively. If you have practiced one of the following exercises you will be even more successful at accomplishing this task.

## 1) Breathing Control Training

Sit comfortably, feet flat on the floor, arms uncrossed in a space that is free from distractions. Allow a 5 minute practice time for this exercise. Close your eyes and shift your focus of concentration to your breathing. Inhale to a slow count of 4, pause, then exhale to a slightly faster count of 7 or 8. As you inhale be sure that you are filling up your abdominal area. To ensure this you may want to place one hand on your diaphragm and feel it rise and fall with your breathing. Repeat this process of inhaling to a slow 4 count and exhaling to the 8 count. Every time you find your mind drifting, quickly and gently bring yourself back to your breathing and **INTERNAL** counting.

### 2) Breathing By 3

Preparation and practice time are the same as #1. Inhale to a slow count of three...pause to a slow count of three, exhale to a slow count of three, pause to a slow count of three. Continue this sequence for the 5 minute period focusing on your breathing and counting. It is not necessary in this exercise to deliberately deepen your breathing. Be sure that you are quick to catch yourself drifting and return to your breathing and counting focus.

### 3) Breathing Meditation

Preparation and practice time are the same as #1. For this exercise you simply focus your concentration on your breathing. You can keep your attention on the rise and fall of your diaphragm or on the air going into and out of your nose and mouth. Your breathing is **NOT** altered at all for this exercise. Distractions should be handled as in #1 and #2. Mentally this exercise involves simply "watching" your breathing.

# Coping Strategy #6 • Music

Many players have learned to handle the pressure of big game competition by listening to certain kinds of music before the game starts. Music can have a powerful effect on your level of arousal. Soft, classical music can soothe you and calm you down while fast-paced rock or rap can pump you up. You can use music by plugging yourself into a walkman, or putting a tune in your head. Oftentimes music will be more effective in raising or lowering your arousal levels if you have picked it out ahead of time and have used it frequently. If you always play the same soft music in the background while you are doing any of the above relaxation techniques, that music by itself will very quickly calm you down under stress.

# Coping Strategy #7 • Visualization

Many players use their imagination to help them manage the negative effects of stress. They mentally leave the stressful environment and "GO" to a relaxing place in their mind's eye. For example, one player will spend the tension filled pre-game time "at the beach" in her mind's eye. This is where she feels most safe and relaxed. Another player will mentally go to a special "relaxation room" just before he takes his penalty kicks. In his "room" he is able to mentally shut the door to any distractions or attempts to psyche him out. A third player takes himself to his practice field where there is no crowd and no tension.

By mentally leaving the stressful environment and going to a **FAMILIAR** and **COMFORTABLE** place, you can effectively calm yourself down pre-game or between the first and second half. **WHAT IS** critical here is that you **REGULARLY** spend time **PRACTICING** going to these relaxing places. This is the **ONLY** way they will work for you when you need them.

## Preparation:

Find a quiet place that is free from distractions where you will be undisturbed for 10-15 minutes. Sit or lie comfortably making sure that your arms and legs are uncrossed. Close your eyes and, using your imagination and memory, mentally take yourself to a relaxing place. **SEE**, **HEAR** and **FEEL** in as much detail as possible what it is like to be in this relaxing place. What familiar things can you see? Are there colors or movement you can make out? **WHAT IS** the lighting like? What kinds of sounds, if any, are part of this place? Are they loud or soft? Close to you or far away? What kind of feelings are you aware of in this place? Can you feel the warmth of the sun on part of your body, or maybe a gentle breeze? You may even want to "construct" a door or passageway to this relaxing place that you can close off to everyone and everything else.

# PRE-GAME COPING STRATEGIES

The above exercises will help you develop and master the skill of relaxation. With sufficient practice you will soon be able to keep yourself calm and composed regardless of the pressure of the moment. For these techniques to consistently work for you it is critical that you practice them regularly, long **BEFORE** you find yourself in that stressful game situation. Pick any two of these to develop as your own.

The following **PRE-GAME** coping techniques can also be used to help you stay calm under pressure. They can be applied **WHILE** you are "Under the gun" to help you stay in control.

### #1 Change Negative Self-Talk

What you say to yourself pre-game/pre-kick will directly effect how nervous you become. If you are talking trash to yourself before a game, or after you make a mistake, you will only stress yourself out. Instead, make a conscious effort to interrupt the flow of negative chatter by replacing it with a more positive inner dialogue. You have to act as your own "**BEST FAN**" while you are on the pitch. Getting down on yourself will only bring your game down!

### #2 Focus on What You Want to Have Happen Not What You Are Afraid Will Happen

Keep your game focus on exactly how you want to play and what you want to do. If you focus on what you are afraid might happen you will not only distract yourself, but you will also stress yourself out even more. If you are setting up to take a penalty kick your focus should be on where you want to put that ball, **NOT** on the consequences of missing the shot. When you are marking your man, your focus should be on how you want to successfully contain him, **NOT** on the embarrassment you will feel if you are beaten.

### #3 Concentrate on Playing the Game. Not On Winning.

If you want to play your very best and win, you must be sure that you [...]
NOT concentrate on winning. Your game focus of attention should never be [...]
how important the game is or what is at stake, but on what you have to do to pl[...]
well. Your focus should be on the PROCESS of the match, NOT on the OU[...]
COME. The process is what is going on at any given moment. If you break fre[...]
and have a shot on goal your focus should be on what you have to do to score[...]
NOT on scoring. If you concentrate on the second by second, minute by minute
process of the game, you will maximize your chances of winning.

### #4 Control The Controllable

Related to #3 be sure that you keep your focus on what you can control. If
you get a questionable call, forget it! You can not control the officiating! If you
are getting razzed by an opponent or the crowd, shift your focus back to the
game. You can not control either of these. Trying to control **ANY** uncontrollable
will only get you more uptight.

### #5 Let Your Mistakes Go Quickly

Dwelling on mistakes, a **HUGE** uncontrollable, will stress you out of the
game. When you make a mistake, let it go quickly and get yourself mentally
back in the game with the next play. If you let an opponent beat you and he
scores, dwelling on it will **NOT** get you to play better. Learn from your mistakes
and quickly let them go.

### #6 Tighten and Release

This is a quick version of the PMR exercise above. If you can feel tension in
your arms, legs or back before the game, a quick way to let this tension go is to
deliberately tighten those tense muscles even more. Hold the tension for 10 - 15
seconds, then let it go. Repeating this 2 - 3 times with any tight muscles will usually help you let go of the tension.

### #7 Stretch

If you are mentally uptight before a game, physically stretch. Stretching will
help you release a great deal of tension from your body and will help you get
back in control.

### #8 Have Fun

If you want to play the best soccer you are capable of, the one word that will
help you do just that is **FUN**. You will **ALWAYS** play your best when you are
having fun. If you make the match so important and so scary that you get too
serious, your performance will suffer. This is one of the main reasons why so
many players choke in big games. Whether you are playing in a minor game or

ship, having fun will insure that you stay loose, run fast and play
_o into their games knowing this. **DO NOT WAIT UNTIL YOU
_ BEFORE YOU HAVE FUN. HAVE FUN FIRST AND YOU
_ WELL.**

_y players, joking around or laughing with friends before the game
_ stay loose. Thinking about the importance of the match and what will
they lose gets them uptight. If you are this kind of player, let yourself
_joy the game and your teammates. Having fun and laughing before the
_ill help you play your best, as long as it does not distract you from the

## ping with "Not Enough" Nervousness

If you or your teammates go into a game under-aroused, that is **TOO**
_nfident and **TOO** cocky, then chances are you could be heading for a huge
all. The overconfident player is a vulnerable player and rarely will he perform to
his potential. The biggest upsets in soccer happen when the stronger team goes
into the game on the wrong side of the curve, in "Not enough" nervousness.

The scenario is a familiar one. Team A is the defending state champions, a
squad full of studs! They have been effortlessly rolling over the opposition. They
like to talk a lot of trash. They see themselves headed for Championship status.
They are feeling and acting "bigger than life". Now they have to play Team B, in
last place in the league standings, a team they shut out 5-0 just 3 weeks ago. This
is going to be a real "Easy" game. Their overconfidence and under-arousal is
going to cost them!

Feeling too cocky, the players on A are totally unprepared for team B's
"We've got nothing to lose" attitude. In the very first minute of play, a striker on
B breaks free and scores. Team B gets even more pumped. Our heroes on A are
in shock as dreams of the Championship and Hall of Fame status quickly shatter.
The remainder of the half is evenly fought and this is taking a toll on A. At the
start of the second half, the players on A come out and try to make something
happen. They are suddenly alarmed and begin to try too hard. Their forcing causes them to make mistakes and, miraculously, B manages to score again. More
Panic sets in on A as the players look for scapegoats to blame. They begin to
fight among themselves and before you know it B scores again. End result:
Upset of the year.

Go into a game too calm and at best you will play totally uninspired and win,
at worst you will panic like the players on A and suffer a humiliating upset! If
you recognize that you are into "not enough" nervousness before a game there
are some things that you can do to get you back up on the curve:

# Psyche-Up Strategies

## #1 Change Your Self-Talk

It is important for you to find a way to increase the importance of the game. One way to do this is by changing the things you say to yourself about the contest. Inner comments like: "this will be a cake walk" and "here comes a real no brainer" will not exactly get you nervous or pumped. Instead you need to challenge yourself: these are the kinds of games that can easily get away from you mentally, "Last year we got upset by a team just like this one", etc. Your task here is very clear: Make yourself more anxious!

## #2 Change Your Goals for the Game

If the outcome of the contest is obvious before it starts, then **DO NOT** have winning as a goal. Challenge yourself with other performance related individual and team goals. i.e. achieving a shut out; keeping control of the game's tempo; beating your opponent to **EVERY** ball; controlling the ball with one touch, etc. Set up ahead of time a way to challenge and stretch your performance that is unrelated to the final score.

## #3 Build-Up the Mental Importance of the Match

You may have your opponent beaten on paper. Your team may be physically and technically superior. There may be little to no real physical challenge for you. Your challenge, instead, is a **MENTAL** one. These are the very hardest games to get up for mentally. Playing a weaker team makes you vulnerable to lapses in intensity and concentration. You may not respect the physical challenge presented by your opponent. Respect the mental one! As in the above example with teams A & B, if you do not win the mental game, you will not win the actual one. Go into the game and keep your focus there.

## #4 Use Simulation to Change the Game and Increase the Challenge

One way to get yourself "UP" for this kind of lop-sided contest is to view it as a rehearsal for a much bigger game. You have to use your imagination and see this game as a warm-up against a much tougher opponent. View every game situation as a test. Challenge yourself the way you know you will be challenged by this other team. Keep your intensity up for every ball. Imagine how that stronger opponent would handle each play. "Forget" who you are actually playing and instead compete against that much tougher opponent.

## #5 Get Yourself Physically "Up"

One way to increase your level of arousal is by increasing your physical movements pre-game. When you are not up for a game there is a tendency to get physically lethargic, to sit or lie around before the game, to move slowly, etc.

Counteract this by acting "Hyper." Stand-up, jump around, get physically "Hyper". In warm-ups push yourself hard. Do not let your mental lethargy get into you physically. If you can get physically "Hyper", your level of arousal will also increase.

# Chapter 4 • Developing Championship Concentration

Your ability to **FOCUS** in on **WHAT IS** important and **BLOCK** out everything else is absolutely essential to reaching your potential as a player. If you can not handle the pressure of performance or if you concentrate on the wrong things at the wrong time you will never play championship soccer.

**CONCENTRATION** is one of **THE** key mental skills responsible for athletic excellence. A mentally tough player is someone who knows HOW to concentrate and can do it under pressure. "Head cases" are those players who can not control their focus of concentration when it counts. Show me a team in a slump and I will show you a group of athletes who have the wrong focus of concentration. Show me a player who chokes or frequently gets psyched out and I will show you someone whose focus **DIRECTLY** causes his problems. A botched penalty kick is almost certainly caused by poor concentration.

Like every other skill area in this book, concentration can be learned and fine tuned with sufficient and proper practice. Remember, in order to develop any skill area, your very first step is to become aware of what you are doing **NOW** that may be getting you into trouble. This is where we will start. But first, let us find out what concentration is all about:

**CONCENTRATION IS A TWO PART SKILL:**

**#1 YOU MUST CATCH YOURSELF WHEN YOU ARE MENTALLY LOSING YOUR FOCUS OR DRIFTING OFF.**

**#2 YOU MUST QUICKLY AND GENTLY BRING YOURSELF BACK TO THE RIGHT FOCUS.**

**CONCENTRATION IS A PARADOXICAL SKILL**. You learn to concentrate by catching yourself when you are **NOT** concentrating and then bringing yourself back.

**CONCENTRATION IS A PASSIVE, LET-IT-HAPPEN SKILL**. You concentrate with "effortless effort". When you are concentrating well you are **NOT** thinking about it, you are just doing it. When you sit for two hours through a great movie you are concentrating intently the entire time. You do not leave the theater soaking wet with sweat and exhausted from your mental efforts to stay focused! It was easy and effortless. You can not make yourself concentrate any more than you can make yourself fall asleep at night.

# The Biggest Mental Mistake made by Players and How You Can Avoid It!

This section of the book can make you a much better player! Poor performance is very often caused by faulty concentration. The biggest cause of choking, missed penalty kicks, psyche-outs and intimidation is when a player violates the **HERE AND NOW RULE** for peak performance.

## The Here and Now Rule For Peak Performance.

This rule states that: **YOU WANT TO DO WHAT YOU ARE DOING MENTALLY WHILE YOU ARE DOING IT PHYSICALLY**.

Very simply, while you are stretching out or warming up pre-game you want to be mentally focused on this rather than the size of your opponents' thighs or awesome abilities. This means that as you set up to take a penalty kick physically, you want to be setting up mentally as well. Thinking about the last penalty kick you blew or the keeper making a save is **NOT** doing mentally what you are doing physically.

More simply, the **HERE** and **NOW RULE** means that you want to **MENTALLY** be in the **HERE** and **NOW** as you play. This rule has two dimensions: **TIME** and **PLACE**.

## Mental Time

Whenever you perform physically you can always be in one of three **TIME ZONES** mentally. You can be in the **PAST**, focused on what just happened, the last time you played this team, an upsetting incident that took place before the game, or an injury you suffered two months ago. You can be in the **NOW** focused on what you are doing at that moment or you can be in the **FUTURE**. Thinking or worrying about what **WILL** happen, "What if I let another goal in", "What if I get cut", "What do I say if we lose" etc.

Whenever you perform physically you can be in one of two general places **MENTALLY**: The **HERE** or the **THERE**. Being in the **HERE** mentally means that you are focusing on **WHAT YOU ARE DOING** and nothing else. It means that you are totally focused on the ball and the developing play as you bring it up field and **NOT** on the coaches on the sideline and what **THEY** may think of your chances of making the select team! Being in the **THERE** mentally means that you are focusing anywhere **EXCEPT** on what you are doing. For example, as the keeper you are listening to and becoming upset by the crowd's razzing. Mentally when you have this focus you are no longer in the goal. Or, as you set up to take the penalty kick you are thinking about how huge the keeper is. Mentally you are in the net, not over the ball the way you should be!

If you violate the **HERE** and **NOW** rule whenever you practice and play you will be sabotaging your game. You will not get as much out of practice and you will play poorly when it counts. Your first job is to quickly recognize when you leave the here and now and then mentally bring yourself back to a proper focus. **AWARENESS IS THE KEY**.

## Recognizing A Past Focus

Phrases like "Here we go again", "I knew this was going to happen", "This ALWAYS happens", and "WE CAN NOT win the big ones", all reflect a past focus. During a game, if you are still thinking about a lousy call or an incredibly lucky save their keeper made, you are in the past and about to make a mistake! You must LET IT GO and get back in the game. Champions do this well. Whenever they make mistakes they quickly rebound and re-focus on the NOW of the match.

## Recognizing A Future Focus

You know that you are mentally time traveling when you hear yourself get into the "what ifs" .i.e. What if I choke, what if they score, what if I get hurt again. Any thoughts about the match's outcome are future. What you will do in the second half, after the game or in the next game are all **FUTURE**. You can not control the future any more than you can get the past back. They are both uncontrollable and your focus on them will take you right out of the game, **FIRST MENTALLY**, and then **PHYSICALLY**!

## Recognizing a "There" Focus

Have you ever been psyched-out or intimidated? Who hasn't! The major cause of these stress reactions is your focus of concentration on someone or something else. To play your best soccer you need to STAY WITHIN YOUR-SELF. You need to keep your focus on what YOU are doing. Thinking about the referee, the crowd, your coach, the keeper or an opponent WHILE you should be bringing the ball up the field is being in the wrong mental place. There is NO way a keeper can intimidate you before a penalty kick unless you CHOOSE to pay attention to HIM! You can only get psyched out if you mentally leave the "Here" and focus "There", on someone or something else.

## For Championship Concentration Control Your Eyes and Ears

If you **CONTROL** what you **LOOK AT** and **LISTEN TO** before and during the game, you will play much better soccer. **CONTROLLING YOUR EYES** pre-game means: Only look at those things that keep you calm, composed and confident. If watching your opponents warm up makes you anxious, control your eyes by looking somewhere else. Focus on your stretching, look at a ball, or pick a spot in front of you to look at. **CONTROLLING YOUR EARS** pre-game means: Only listen to things (outside or internal) that keep you calm, composed and confident. If someone in the crowd is picking on you, listen to something else. Put a tune in your head. Focus on a positive internal dialogue. If you are picking on yourself with negative self-talk, go talk to someone on the team, change the negative to positive, or otherwise distract yourself from that nasty chatter.

Do not wait until a tense situation before you start looking around for things to look at or listen to. **BE PREPARED**! Figure out ahead of time the things you can use to keep your eyes away from tension producing stimuli. Do the same in relation to your auditory focus. Have a pre-game or pre-kick plan you can use to help yourself stay focused.

## Using Focal Points to Control Your Eyes

One technique is to develop specific focal points for each game you play. **BEFORE** the game, preferably before anyone else is on the field, pick out 2-3 specific **FOCAL POINTS** you can look at when things get tough. These focal points can be anywhere around the field, but should be easily spotted by you. i.e. a tree on the sideline, part of the bleachers, one of the goal posts, etc.

You can even assign a special meaning to that focal point, so that when you look at it you are reminded of that meaning. For example, your focal point can remind you that: "You have paid your physical dues and are ready", "You belong on this team and can play with the best of them", "You are mentally and physically tougher than everyone out here", etc.

If you are about to play in a big championship game and have never played in front of a huge crowd before, you can use your focal points to help you stay calm for this match. Pick several out before the crowd arrives and you are still relatively calm. Once the stadium or bleachers begin to fill and the tension builds you can then keep yourself composed by controlling your eyes and concentrating on your focal points.

## Letting Go of the Past - Dealing with Mistakes and Bad Breaks.

You are only as good as your ability to play the game in the **HERE** and **NOW**. If you are mentally in the **PAST** or **FUTURE** while you perform, your play will suffer. One of the hardest things for a soccer player to learn is to mentally let go of the **PAST**. You make a mistake, get beaten by an opponent, or let a goal score if you are the keeper, and it just eats at you! If you hang onto a mistake, I promise you that more will follow. Mistakes are part of this game. **EVERYONE** makes them. You have to learn to **FORGIVE** yourself and then **FORGET**! Here is a technique or two that you can use to help leave the mistakes where they belong, **IN THE PAST**!

# Developing a Mistake Ritual • Goalkeepers

This is **ONLY** appropriate for the keeper because he is the only one with enough **TIME**. If you are a perfectionist and have no tolerance for your mistakes you may find this especially useful. Your opponents score on you and you feel angry and responsible. What is your mental task? To **LEAVE THE MISTAKE BEHIND AND GET BACK IN THE GAME**! If you practice the following little ritual (you can change it in any way you like) it will help you let go of your frustration and anger so you can get back in the game.

It starts with the goal being scored. Turn your back on the ball and walk off to the side of the net. Bend down and pick up a handful of grass. The grass will symbolically represent your mistake. After every mistake you have 3 tasks:

**1) SWITCH YOUR FOCUS AWAY FROM THE MISTAKE** - Usually when a keeper lets a goal in he will keep thinking about how he made a mistake. This focus will undermine your confidence, raise your anxiety to a performance inhibiting level, tighten you up physically and distract your concentration from the game.

**2) CHANGE YOUR NEGATIVE SELF-TALK** - After you make a mistake there is a good chance you will begin to get hard on yourself. This does nothing for your confidence and only makes you more uptight. What is important is that you replace the negative with positive.

**3) GET CONTROL OF YOUR AROUSAL LEVEL** - When you make a mistake you get more uptight. You can not play well when you are tense so it is crucial that you control your level of arousal after you make mistakes.

While you are looking at the grass, task 1, distracting yourself from the mistake with a visual focus, you want to begin to change your negative self talk, task 2, i.e. Let it go "you will get it back", stay in the **NOW** "she got lucky", etc. While you are changing the negative self-talk you also want to begin to take several, slow diaphragmatic breaths, task 3, calming yourself down.

When you have finished this little ritual, it should take you no more than 10 seconds or so, you want to then throw away the grass, the mistake, and **WALK AWAY FROM IT**. Then get back in the goal and get set.

# Letting Go of Mistakes - Field Players Mistake Cue

Unfortunately field players do not have the luxury of getting play to stop whenever they screw up so that they can go through a little mistake ritual. Play will not stop for you! However, mentally you must do exactly what the keeper does! You must quickly leave your mistake behind you. One way to remind yourself of this is to DEVELOP A MISTAKE CUE, something that will help you let go of the mistake or accompanying emotions. Saying things like "Let go", "Cancel", "Erase", "Now" etc. can serve as your split second mistake ritual. If you practice letting go of mistakes **DURING PRACTICE** with **ONE** of these cues, ultimately it will work for you in a game. One coach I worked with developed the word "cancel" as the team's mistake cue. Everyone on the squad knew what it meant and knew what to do whenever he heard "cancel" from the coach, the keeper or another field player.

# Fist Squeeze

There is a physical feeling you can recognize in your body of letting go. Crumple up a piece of paper in your hand or hold some other soft object like a sock, sponge or rubber ball. Stand with your arms by your sides and the paper or object in one hand. Close your eyes and squeeze your hand as tightly as possible around that soft object. Hold the tension for 10 seconds and then say "Let go" to yourself (or the cue word that you will use to represent letting go) and as you do, slowly allow your fingers to relax around the object until you let it fall to the floor. **REPEAT** this process several times, focusing carefully on the feelings in your arm and hand of "Letting go." **NEXT**, think of something that you messed up that day, either at school, at work or in practice. As you focus on the **PAST** images of your mistake, squeeze the object and imagine that you are holding onto that mistake very tightly. Then, repeat your "let go" cue to yourself and as you feel those familiar physical feelings of "letting go" up and down your arm, let go of those mistake images and thoughts. Practice the fist squeeze technique and you may be surprised to find that you can use it effectively **DURING** the game.

# Mistake Waste Basket

Another mental trick that can help you quickly get back in the game, is developing one or more "Mistake waste baskets" around the pitch. Before the game pick a few spots around the field that you will designate as your mistake receptacles. Whenever you screw up and can not seem to let go of it, imagine that you can quickly "deposit" the faux pas into one of those wastebaskets. if you want to "retrieve" the mistake **AFTER** the game so you can work on it, fine. But, **DURING** the match is not the time to dwell on your mistakes.

# Championship Concentration • Pre-Game and for Penalty Kicks

If you are concentrating on the **WRONG** things before a game or as you get set to take a penalty kick you will be unknowingly setting yourself up for failure. As I mentioned, your job in both of these situations is to mentally stay in the

**HERE** and **NOW**. But what does that really mean? How do you do that? The main way to stay in the here and now is by controlling your eyes and ears, by having specific things that you do or focus on which you use to deliberately **DISTRACT YOU FROM ALL THE OTHER DISTRACTIONS**.

Your concentration is limited. At any given time you can only concentrate on a set number of things. Furthermore, while you may be able to focus on a few things at the same time, **YOU CAN REALLY ONLY FOCUS ON ONE THING WELL AT A TIME**. If you are concentrating on "Garbage" ("These guys are awesome", "What if I miss", "Last game I missed an open goal") you have less room in your head to focus on the things that will insure you play well. Therefore it is critical that what you focus on is performance enhancing. How do you do this pre-game? How do you do this before penalty kicks?

# Using Rituals to Develop Winning Concentration • Pre-Game

Diagram #2 represents your pre-game or pre-kick concentration and how it must change as the time for performance approaches. The left side of the chart represents the time before the game. 15-30 minutes before the game your concentration can be broad. You can be thinking about a lot of different things. However, as the time of the start approaches, you must begin to **NARROW** your concentration (moving left to right on the chart) until you have a one point focus as the game starts. The way that you can stay in the **HERE** and **NOW**, and progressively narrow your focus of attention is by going through a set pre-game ritual. Every great athlete in every sport goes through the **SAME** routine before every performance.

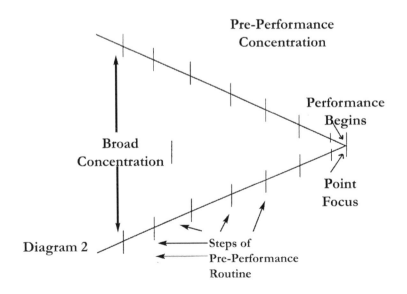

Diagram 2

Pre-Performance Concentration

Performance Begins

Point Focus

Broad Concentration

Steps of Pre-Performance Routine

50

Your ritual can include a pre-game meal (or not), getting suited up for the game ("I am putting on my championship shoes") or simply start 5-10 minutes before the match. It may involve a set way of stretching, taking off warm-ups, juggling, dribbling, particular music, cracking knuckles, pacing etc. It really does not matter **WHAT** is in your pre-game ritual as long as these are things that YOU can control. Sometimes athletes develop superstitions and rituals that they can not always repeat. For example, having to eat a certain pre-game meal and this food is unavailable in the area. Your rituals should involve things and actions that you know you can always do, (i.e. putting on and lacing your shoes in a certain way, doing specific stretches, handling a ball, etc.)

Further, it is critical that as you do the rituals you stay in the **HERE** and the **NOW**. Remember, the purpose of the ritual is to help you stay centered, to stay calm and focused. The ritual is a way that you can distract yourself from all of the pressures and distractions surrounding you. If you are out on the field stretching (as part of your ritual), but mentally you are thinking about how awesome the other team is, you are **NOT** in the here and now. In this example your ritual is **NOT** serving its focusing function. Whenever you catch this happening, remember to recognize that you are in the wrong mental place or time, and then quickly bring yourself back.

# Using Rituals to Develop Winning Concentration Pre-Penalty Kick

When any decent player misses a penalty kick it is mainly a **MENTAL** thing. Specifically, the shooter has made a concentration mistake. He has failed to stay in the **HERE** and **NOW** of the shooting situation. He has been distracted by the keeper, the crowd or his own past ("Last time I...) or future ("What if...) thoughts. Having a set pre-kick ritual is a must for success here. Without a good ritual you have no way to effectively narrow your concentration the way it needs to be for you to maximize your chances of a goal.

As a field player, you must be able to quickly shift your concentration during the game. You must have a **BROAD EXTERNAL** focus which takes in the entire field, any developing plays, on-coming defenders and the location of your teammates. If you break away and have an opportunity to score, you need to begin to narrow your concentration to the keeper and the net. Finally when you go to score, or control the ball, you **MUST** have a **NARROW EXTERNAL** focus on the ball.

If you are going to take a penalty kick, you have to be able to have this **NARROW EXTERNAL** focus. You have to pick a spot where you are going to go and then turn your attention inward on the ball and where you will hit it. This is why having a set pre-shot ritual is so critical for taking penalty kicks. It helps you as a shooter narrow your concentration and block out any distractions from the crowd or psyche-out attempts from the keeper. Keep in mind, however, you must be in the here and now **AS** you go through the ritual. If you are thinking about the keeper and what he might do, you are in the wrong mental place. You must quickly recognize this and bring yourself back to your ritual.

# Exercises to Develop Winning Concentration

**PREPARATION:** For all exercises, begin by sitting comfortably in a place where you will not be distracted. After gaining proficiency in your ability to concentrate you can progressively add distractions. Allow 5 minutes for each exercise unless otherwise indicated.

### #1 • Ball Stare

Place a ball directly in front of you and focus your attention on it. Study it carefully, examining the stitching, colors and writing. As you watch it, slowly repeat to yourself the word "Ball". Quickly bring your focus back to the ball every time you find yourself drifting. Next, close your eyes and try to get a visual image of the ball. Continue to repeat "Ball" to yourself as you do this. Finally, pick the ball up and study it with your hands. Feel the texture of the surfaces, the seams, the temperature of the leather, etc., and as you do this continue to repeat "Ball" to yourself. Repeat this sequence (looking, imaging and feeling) for 5 minutes.

### #2 • Blocking Distractions

Sit up close to your TV screen with the set on and no volume. Hold your thumb out against the screen and focus only on the center of your thumbnail for about 10 seconds. When you can do this without being distracted by the pictures, increase your time to 20 seconds. When you can go a whole minute, turn the volume up and try to focus only on your thumb for 10 seconds without being distracted by the sound or pictures. Continue to increase your time until you can go 12 minutes without losing your focus.

### #3 • Bring Yourself Back • The Heart of Championship Concentration

Focus your attention on your breathing as you inhale. With each exhalation switch your focus to the number "1", you can repeat the sound to yourself or "See" a number "1" in your mind's eye. Inhale, focus on your breathing; exhale, focus on the number "1." When you first find your mind distracted or wandering, gently return to your focus in the following way: Concentrate on the feeling of the inhale. As you exhale focus now on the number "2". With each distraction, recognize you are drifting, bring yourself back and increase the number you focus on by one.

# Chapter 5 • Thinking Like A Winner - Developing a Positive Attitude

If you want to become a winner on the field, you have to first learn to **THINK** like one! The great soccer players have a different way of thinking than everyone else. They maintain a different attitude. They look at obstacles and problems in a way that builds their confidence and inspires their play. Very simply, they think like winners.

How do **YOU** develop winning thinking? What if you are the kind of player who is incredibly negative...is there hope for you? **YES**!!

Like every other topic in this training manual, winning thinking is a **LEARNED** skill. With regular practice and persistence even **YOU** can turn that negative attitude around and start to use your head to play better. But you must be patient! Anything worth learning does **NOT** happen overnight!

The heart of winning thinking is being positive. Winners know that **NOTH-ING GOOD COMES FROM BEING NEGATIVE.** When you are negative or down on yourself, your teammates, your coach or anything else, you are sapping your energy, eroding your confidence and setting yourself up for failure. When one member of a team is negative, he can bring the whole squad down with him. Negativity goes hand in hand with failure. If you **REALLY** want to become a champion, then you must understand that there is no room in your training for a negative attitude.

Negativity will **NOT** help you win a game you are losing. Positive thinking is the stuff of comebacks! Negativity will not help you recover from a tough loss. Positive thinking will get you back on track fast! Negativity will **NOT** make you a popular player on the team. A positive attitude will win friends and help create a cohesive winning team. When you are injured, negativity will slow your rehabilitation and turn you into a tentative player when you can play again. Maintaining a positive attitude will not only help you make the best of that physical setback, but will get you back to your old playing form quicker.

## Losers are Negative, Winners are Positive. You Choose the Attitude, the Attitude Creates the Results!!!

So **HOW** can you begin to practice and develop winning thinking? Let us start by reviewing what I called "The uncontrollable" in soccer, the factors, situations and things that are totally out of your direct control. The uncontrollables are: weather, playing conditions, field, crowd, opponents, officiating, winning, losing, past, future, coach, teammates, etc. The only controllable thing in all of these factors is **YOUR** reaction to all of them. This is where winning thinking comes in.

There are basically two ways you can look at these uncontrollables when they occur. 1. You can look at them negatively. You can use them to **UNDER-CUT** your confidence and as an excuse for why you will not play well. Negative people are **ALWAYS** making excuses for their failures. 2. You can look at them positively. You can use them to **ENHANCE** your confidence and give yourself the competitive edge. Positive people **NEVER** stop looking for ways to get better.

Having a positive winning attitude means that when adversity looks you straight in the eye, you smile and say "Thank you very much for this wonderful opportunity!" This is the mental skill of **RE-FRAMING**. Re-framing is a way of viewing the uncontrollable. Re-framing means "When life gives you lemons, you make lemonade!" **WHEN OBSTACLES GET THROWN IN YOUR PATH YOU FIND A WAY TO USE THEM TO HELP YOU GO FASTER AND GET STRONGER.**

In late November, 1987 the University of Massachusetts women's soccer team hosted the NCAA Final Four. That weekend, the weather was unseasonably cold. With the temperature in the single digits and a steady 40 mph wind which registered a wind chill of about 20 below, U Mass got set to play their semifinal match against Central Florida.

The on field playing conditions were brutal to say the least. The ground was frozen rock hard, the wind was relentless and powerful, and the cold cut through you like a knife. Even running around on the field did little to warm the players. Each team had an "opportunity" to use these dreadful weather conditions in their favor **OR** to their disadvantage.

I spoke to the University of Massachusetts women before this game and they talked about how awful the game conditions were and how difficult it was going to be to control the ball. Then we talked about re-framing and how they could use the wind and the cold as a boost. I explained that **NO ONE** likes playing in these conditions, least of all players from the state of Florida! I encouraged the players to consider the effect the weather was going to have on their opponents. Sub-zero temperatures and strong winds was U Mass's weather and would bother the Central Floridians **MUCH** more than it would the Minute women. I asked them to see themselves as mentally and physically tougher to handle the weather. Then I asked them to remember what this kind of weather does to Florida's prize fruit, the orange. This is what re-framing is all about. The U Mass women went out and dominated their opponents to win easily. Having a positive attitude about the lousy playing conditions helped the team maintain their intensity and spirit.

Recently I spoke to a high school coach who did a similar thing with his girl's team. He noticed that his players always came out tentatively whenever they had to compete in the rain. The younger players especially seemed to be reluctant to get themselves muddy right away. After the first half when they were covered with mud they loosened up and played aggressively.

His solution to this "Problem" involved a bit of re-framing. Everyone knows that rain and mud make you play better, if you re-frame them. So this coach had his team regularly get muddy **BEFORE** their matches to get a quick "Edge". Before a big tournament, with the rain coming down heavily and the middle of the field a small lake, he had his players go through their "Mud game" routine. One at a time, they ran out to the center field mud puddles and, in front of the opposing team, dove right into the mud covering themselves completely! Then they went out and smothered their opponents throughout the game.

This strange pre-game mud ritual communicates a powerful message to an opponent. We love this weather and play well in it. In other words it gave the team a powerful psychological boost.

Because of a low budget and apathetic administration, a high school boy's team was forced to practice and play on a field that could have easily passed as an obstacle course. The pitch was covered with potholes, discarded trash and everything except grass. The players spent a great deal of time using this uncontrollable to undermine their spirit and confidence. They complained that the other teams in the league had an unfair advantage over them because each of their opponents got to practice on a real soccer field.

This is where the coach stepped in to do a little re-framing. During one of their more vocal complaint sessions he told them he did not want to hear another negative word about the field. Besides, he explained, they had it all backwards. **THEIR** field gave **THEM** an unfair advantage over their opponents. Of course his players became totally confused by his response, so he explained, "As of today I am renaming our field The Lion's Den, (the team's nickname was the lions)...Now do you boys know what happens in a lion's den?...Great things if you are a lion! Not so great things if you are an 'Invited guest!' **EVERY** team that comes to our 'Den' to play us is going to have trouble with this pitch. They will be distracted by it and complain about it. This is your field. You guys are mentally tougher than anyone in the league when it comes to playing under this kind of adversity! Furthermore, if you guys can play on this field, you can play **ANYWHERE**! When you play away, you will have an easy time adjusting to decent field conditions."

Re-framing is a skill in which you practice taking the negative, potentially confidence eroding things that happen to you, and turn them into a positive. The uncontrollables effect **BOTH** you and your opponent. Give yourself the edge by using adversity in your favor.

Re-framing takes practice and may not come naturally at first. However, every dis---**ADVANTAGE** has an advantage in it. Every problem presents you with an opportunity. This is what re-framing is all about and this is the heart of winning thinking. Start right now to train yourself to look for the positive. Being negative is easy. It takes no particular skills or energy and it is what losers do best. **NOTHING GOOD COMES FROM BEING NEGATIVE**! Be a winner. Make re-framing an integral part of your game.

# Exercise

Take 15 - 20 minutes at home to do the following exercise: Think about all the uncontrollables in practice or game situations that you have used negatively to undermine your confidence. Write each of these down. Next, think about how you could have **RE-FRAMED** each of these as a positive. For example, towards the end of the game your play suffers and confidence slips because of fatigue. A re-frame of fatigue would be: "I am totally exhausted, but so is everyone else out here right now, and I am mentally and physically tougher than my opponent."

In the beginning it may be difficult for you to re-frame a negative in the middle of a game. However, if you go through this exercise several times a week you will soon develop this habit. One of the best times to work on this is immediately **AFTER** a game. Review what happened and think about which situations you could have re-framed in your favor.

# Chapter 6:
# Developing Self-Confidence

If you want to reach your potential as a player and go as far as you can in this sport you need self-confidence to help you get there. Physical talent, strength, speed and endurance are not enough. You have to believe in yourself and your abilities. You have to develop the inner "Knowing" of what self-confidence is all about. It is what you see and hear in every great player. Inside they **KNOW** they are good. They feel it, believe it, walk it and sometimes talk it.

Most people think self-confidence is something that comes from success. First you have success, then naturally your self-confidence will follow. This is **NOT** how it works. Yes, experiencing successes is an important part of developing self-confidence. It is difficult to feel good about yourself and believe in your abilities if you experience nothing but failure. However, I have seen too many soccer players who have had tremendous successes, yet feel little confidence. On paper you'd think these players would feel on top of the world. Instead, they claim they are plagued by selfdoubts and do not think they are so good.

Years ago I worked with a nationally ranked swimmer who was a case in point. Much of what he had experienced in his competitive career was success. His failures were few and far between. Strangely this swimmer did not really believe he was that good. He did not feel or show the kind of self-confidence you would expect. **WHY**?

This athlete and too many like him got me thinking about how self-confidence is developed. You learn to feel good or bad about yourself depending on how you **INTERPRET** your successes and failures. An objective success does not necessarily mean that your self-confidence will rise. You can win a game for your team with a last second goal and still come away from that match feeling like a loser. **HOW**?

If you succeed at something and afterwards explain your success away, i.e. "I was lucky", "They didn't have their good players on the field", etc. then you will end up robbing yourself of the good feelings that go into developing self-confidence. Players who do not believe in themselves do this regularly. They downplay or minimize their victories. They never give themselves full credit for a job well done. Where others see a success in their performance, this kind of athlete either ignores it or finds a failure. And if for some reason he feels he has done well, he does not allow himself to hang onto those good feelings. He quickly forgets them and begins to think, "I was successful, **BUT** what about next time."

Let us say that in addition to explaining away your successes, you also had a tendency to exaggerate your failures. Your team loses and you blame it on yourself. You look for things that you did wrong and you blow them out of proportion. If you can not find anything, then you make something up. Furthermore, you also hang onto these failures for days. You constantly relive them and remind yourself of your shortcomings. How do you think you will end up feeling? Yes, like **GARBAGE**.

These are the things I have found going on inside of athletes who lack confidence. Even though they had ability and successes, they felt badly about themselves **BECAUSE** of what they did with their successes and failures. Minimize, ignore or explain away your good performances and you will feel crummy. Exaggerate or blow out of proportion your failures and you will feel worse.

If you want to **GROW** self-confidence inside, you must change these inner explanations. You have to give credit where credit is due. You have to begin to act like your own best fan. A good sports fan is one who believes in and supports the team **NO MATTER WHAT** (NMW). When the team goes through a hard luck streak a good fan does not yell from the stands, "Throw the bums out." He gives the support that is needed. Only a "Fair weather" fan does this. He loves you when you are winning and looks for another team to support when you are losing. You can not afford to be a "Fair weather" fan to yourself. Not if you want to become a champion!

In an earlier part of this book I discussed the GIGO factor. **GARBAGE IN = GARBAGE OUT**. Program garbage into a computer and the computer will give you garbage back, i.e. it will not do what you would like it to. Think the wrong thoughts before a game or penalty kick (garbage in) and you will get garbage back in terms of your performance. The GIGO factor works in relation to developing self-confidence. To feel good about yourself you have to "Feed" yourself good stuff. If you are in the habit of explaining away your successes and highlighting your failures, garbage in, then you will have little to no self-confidence, garbage out.

Developing self-confidence is a lot like advertising. What sells a product on TV is the commercial. When you see young, physically fit, attractive actors or actresses drinking a product on location in a beautiful place, it makes you want to go out and get that product. Advertising like that leads you to believe that if you consume the product you too will get everything shown on the screen.

As a consumer you would never buy something that was advertised negatively. If you were told in a TV commercial, for example, that a soft drink rotted your teeth and gave you high blood pressure, and the actors and actresses shown on the screen were fat, ugly and grossly out of shape, it would not make you want to run out and buy a case of the drink. On the contrary! Good advertising always sells a product.

As a soccer player you can use this concept to build your self-confidence. You need to learn to advertise your most important product, **YOU**, to your most important customer, **YOU**! Proving to others that you are good will **NOT** necessarily raise your confidence level. Proving it to yourself **WILL**!

# Developing Confidence

## Exercise #1 • Using Positive Affirmations

You become what you think about most of the time. One way to begin to take control of this principle and build confidence is by using positive statements or affirmations. When you say negative things to yourself you will feel bad. Find an area where you have little confidence and begin to change your negative self statements. Let us say that you fall apart under pressure and regularly trash yourself as a "Choke." Instead, repeat to yourself the affirmation, "I am calm and composed under pressure", or "I love pressure" or "I am a crunch time player." You do not have to believe a word of this in the beginning. All you need to do is write that affirmation down on paper and repeat it to yourself 50-60 times a day, every day for a week or two. Affirmations should be positive and in the present tense.

## Exercise #2 • Self Advertising

Take one or more of the affirmations you are working on and make small 3"x 5" signs. Write down how you want to feel as if it were already true. For example, "I control my emotions under pressure" or "I am a confident powerful striker." Make 5 or 6 (or more) signs for each affirmation. Next, put these signs all around your room, in your changing bag, school books and anywhere you are sure to see them. Focus on these self advertisements as frequently as possible making sure they are the last things you see before bed and the very first things you see when you wake up.

## Exercise #3 • Pre-sleep Technique

Take one affirmation and work on it for at least a week in the following way: After you turn your light off and are lying in bed ready to go to sleep, begin to slowly repeat your affirmation twenty times. Keep count with the fingers of both hands and be sure to get through all 20 before allowing yourself to drift off to sleep.

## Exercise #4 • Victory Log

Keep a journal or log all of your successes. You can include newspaper clippings, letters, comments from coaches or anything else representing the things you have done well. Be sure to **ONLY** log the positive. Re-read your log often, and **ESPECIALLY** when your self-confidence has been shaken.

## Exercise #5 • Wall of Fame

Make a wall in your room a motivational guide. Take news clippings of all your successes, pictures, slogans and anything else you can think of that will constantly remind you of **WHERE** you are going and the **FACT** that you can get there! Be creative with this and remember: **KEEP YOUR VICTORIES AND SUCCESSES DIRECTLY IN FRONT OF YOU. LEARN FROM YOUR FAILURES AND SETBACKS AND THEN FORGET THEM!!!** You want to work on developing a long term memory for your successes and a short term memory for your failures.

## Exercise #6 • Controlling Negative Self-Talk
If you listen to enough garbage about yourself, ultimately you will begin to feel like garbage. Begin to actively stop negative or self-defeating messages by going through the following four step process:

1.  Say "Stop" to yourself the instant you become aware of a negative message.
2. Take a slow deep breath and as you exhale imagine that you can blow that thought away.
3. Re-frame the thought in a positive way. i.e. turn "I always make those mistakes" to "I am learning, let it go."
4. Re-focus your concentration back where it belongs.

# Chapter 7 • Big Game Preparation Using Mental Rehearsal for Peak Performance

## Winners See What They Want to have Happen, Losers See What They Are Afraid Will Happen

Soccer, like many other sports, is a very physical game. There is no question that unless you train your body, your physical skills, strength and endurance, you will never become a champion. You must, **IN ADDITION**, train your mind. That has been the purpose of this book. To be a consistent winner you have to develop the **MIND** of a champion.

One critical area of mental training and preparation that needs to be addressed has to do with visualization and mental rehearsal. In other words, the kind of pictures you make in your mind's eye before you perform. Do you see yourself playing well and doing your job or tripping over your own feet and getting totally humiliated?

**EVERYONE**, whether he is aware of it or not, produces images in his mind in relation to an upcoming performance. If you have a big game in three weeks and you have been thinking about it every day, then every day you have been making images in your mind's eye. Without knowing it you have been mentally rehearsing for that game. This is because mental pictures always accompany the thoughts we have. So what is so important about that?

What is important about the pictures that go floating around in your mind is just this: **IMAGERY PROGRAMS YOUR PERFORMANCES**. The pictures you make in your mind's eye **DIRECTLY** effect **HOW** you will play. If you are worried about messing up, **WATCH OUT**. You may be inadvertently programming yourself to do just that! In other words, to be as successful as possible on the pitch you must learn to monitor and control the kinds of images that you produce in your head.

Remember having a dream so vivid that after you awoke there was a split second or two when you were not sure whether you were dreaming or not. Or perhaps you have had the experience of being bored in school or in a meeting and suddenly found yourself drifting off in a day dream, at the beach or on the pitch. In both of these experiences your mind is able to produce such life-like images that the line between reality and fantasy gets blurry for a short time.

**MENTAL REHEARSAL IS ONE OF THE MOST POWERFUL MENTAL SKILLS YOU CAN USE AS A SOCCER PLAYER TO OVERCOME SETBACKS, EFFECTIVELY HANDLE PRESSURE, AND LIFT THE LEVEL OF YOUR PHYSICAL GAME.**

**MENTAL REHEARSAL** is the systematic creation, or recreation, of images (visual, auditory and kinesthetic) in your mind's eye, which are directly aimed at enhancing performance. Very simply, **IT IS** mental practice! **IT IS** based on the idea that if you want to play like a champion on the pitch, you must first play like one in your mind. You must win mentally before you can win in reality. When practiced correctly and mastered, the **SKILL** of mental rehearsal will make you a mentally tough soccer player and help you make the very best use of your physical talents.

The power of **MENTAL REHEARSAL** is based on the fact that images from your brain serve as blueprints for your actions and behaviors. Think about that vivid dream again. For a brief period, your body responded to that dream as if it were real, increasing your heartbeat, blood pressure, breathing and muscle tension.

In a similar way your body will respond to images that you produce whenever you mentally rehearse a performance, **IF** those images being played in your mind are vivid enough to seem real. The nerves that connect to the particular muscle groups involved in the action you are imagining begin to fire, and the muscles are stimulated to a degree just below actual movement. In this way, the body and muscles can actually be programmed to respond to situations and function in a particular way. It is as though every time the mind creates an image of the action, taking a penalty kick for example, grooves are cut into a record in the brain, grooves that will be followed again later, when that kick is actually performed.

Therefore **IT IS** absolutely critical that you know what "Movies" you are playing in your mind's eye. All too often athletes will feature such nightmares as, **"DO NOT MISS THAT KICK", "THE LAST TIME I HAD TO FACE HER SHE TOTALLY HUMILIATED ME" or "WE CAN NEVER SEEM TO WIN THE BIG GAMES."** Understand that the accompanying imagery with these worrisome thoughts is entirely negative!

If you want to really get those images working **FOR**, not **AGAINST** you, follow these guidelines when you practice the exercises at the end of this section:

### #1 ALL IMAGERY SHOULD BE PRECEDED BY RELAXATION • If

you want your practice sessions to be as useful as possible, you must start them with a brief, 5 minute, period of relaxation. Stress makes the production of constructive imagery nearly impossible. Being relaxed will increase the vividness of your images and thus make them more effective. You can use any arousal control exercise we discussed to help you achieve this relaxed state. This means that, at least until you master the skill, your sessions should always be held in an environment that is free from distractions.

**#2 ALL IMAGERY SHOULD BE AS VIVID OR LIFE-LIKE AS POSSIBLE** • Try to make the images you produce in your mind's eye as vivid and detailed as possible. For visual images you should try to "See" color, movement, lighting, dark or bright, shapes, etc. For sound images you want to "Hear" volume, loud or soft, tones, pitch, etc. For kinesthetic or feeling images you want to "Feel" the pitch underfoot, temperature, texture of the ball, wind in your face, movement as you run for the ball, the emotions of confidence or wild excitement after a score, etc.

**#3 ARE YOU INSIDE OR OUTSIDE THE ACTION?** • There are two perspectives that you can have whenever you practice mental rehearsal. First, you can be **OUTSIDE** the action and "See, feel and hear" what you would if you were a spectator or watching yourself. Second, you can be **INSIDE** the action and "See, hear and feel" what you would if you were on the pitch running after the ball. **INTERNAL** imagery, or being inside the action is said to be most effective in enhancing overall performance. **EXTERNAL** imagery or being outside the action is said to be useful whenever you are working on learning new skills. Experiment with both perspectives, **BUT** be sure that you master the **INTERNAL** one.

**#4 HAVE AN IMAGERY GOAL IN MIND FOR EVERY SESSION** • Physical practice is **ALWAYS** more effective when you have a clear goal in mind and work towards its accomplishment. Mental practice is the same. If you have trouble staying in emotional control whenever you play, focus on this in your practice sessions. Mentally rehearse yourself staying calm and composed no matter what happens on the pitch. If you have trouble with a specific ball control skill or kicking technique for penalty shots, practice these in your mind's eye.

**#5 HAVE A BEGINNING, MIDDLE AND END FOR YOUR SESSIONS** If you are using mental rehearsal to prepare for an upcoming game be sure that your session starts with pre-game imagery, getting dressed, warming-up, the opening minutes of play, etc., make sure it has imagery from the middle of the match, and ends with imagery of the last few minutes of the game as well as the celebration at the end. Use this format whenever you are doing pre-game preparation. If you are merely working on strengthening a particular skill, rebounding quickly from mistakes, staying focused, using the proper kicking technique, this format is not necessary.

**#6 MAKE YOUR PRACTICE SESSIONS SHORT, 10 - 15 MINUTES,** • If you try to spend too much time mentally rehearsing you will have difficulty concentrating and may bore yourself to sleep. More frequent, shorter sessions are much more effective than fewer, longer ones. If you are totally into a mental rehearsal session you can choose to extend its length. However, short is the best rule of thumb.

**#7 BE PATIENT AND PRACTICE** • Imagery is a skill. Mastery takes consistent practice. In the beginning you may find that you can not "See" anything in your mind's eye. This is normal. Think yourself through the action and be patient. With practice you will learn to produce clearer and more life-like images. Understand that you may also not be able to **CONTROL** the images in the beginning. As a keeper, you may start to practice being in a game when suddenly the images have you making mistakes and letting goals in. Learning to **CONTROL YOUR IMAGES** comes with time. Whenever your images come up the wrong way use the **VCR TECHNIQUE**: Pretend you are operating your very own VCR in your mind. Hit the stop button, rewind the pictures and play it again. If it comes up negative a second or third time, do the same. Put it in slow motion if you must in order to get it right. Be patient!!! The pictures will soon come around.

# MENTAL REHEARSAL EXERCISES

**#1 DEVELOPING A PEAK PERFORMANCE CUE, REPLAYING A GREAT GAME** • Think about the last time you had a **GREAT** game! The more emotional the experience was for you, the better. Remember what made that game so special. Close your eyes, and spend 5 minutes allowing yourself to relax. Next, travel back in time to this great performance and begin to "Replay" it in your mind's eye, seeing, hearing and feeling everything that you did. Do so in as much detail as possible.

Once you have gone through the game, find the one point in that match that really captured your "Winning feelings." Focus in on that one play or time when you really felt on top of the world, unstoppable, totally confident. Replay this scene over and over again, paying close attention to the accompanying emotions, confidence, excitement, etc..

Next, think of a **PEAK PERFORMANCE CUE,** a symbol that you can use to remind yourself of these winning feelings. Your symbol can be a word: awesome, tough, power, a phrase: "I am the king of the pitch", "No one can touch me", a color: red, black, an image: a locomotive, mountain lion, or a muscle movement: a clenched fist.

As you review the scene where you feel your winning feelings most intensely, repeat your peak performance cue to yourself. Feel those feelings, repeat your cue. Pair these two, peak performance imagery/feelings with your cue, at least 10 times with each practice session. If you have chosen a game that has a lot of emotion attached to it, soon you will find that just by using your pre-game cue, all of those winning emotions will come back.

**YOU HAVE TO FEEL LIKE A WINNER BEFORE YOU CAN PLAY LIKE ONE**. Developing and using a peak performance cue can help you recapture those past-winning feelings and bring them to your next game.

**#2 PREPARING FOR A BIG GAME - MASTERY IMAGERY** • One of the best ways to prepare yourself for an upcoming match is by regularly "Practicing" that game in your head the weeks and days leading up to it. See, feel and hear **EXACTLY** what you would like to have happen in this game. Focus on the details and process of the match, **NOT** just on winning. Experience yourself playing and executing **JUST** the way you would like to. Feel strong, confident, powerful and perform to the upper limits of your abilities. Imagine and experience the emotions that accompany all these images. Use the imagery guidelines to help you.

**#3 HANDLING PSYCHE - OUTS, OVERCOMING OBSTACLES, REBOUNDING FROM SETBACKS - COPING IMAGERY** • It is the unexpected that will easily knock you off center and spoil your play. It is the negative emotional response that mentally takes you out of the game. Mental rehearsal can help you prepare for these so that when someone or something "pushes your buttons" before or during the game, you play like a champion.

STEP #1 • Make a list of your "Hot buttons", the things that get you upset, angry or emotional, i.e. making mistakes, getting tackled hard, someone talking trash to you, etc..

STEP #2 • Next to each "Hot button", think of 1 or 2 **IDEAL COPING RESPONSES (ICR)**, or the perfect way to respond to that hot button. For example, retaliating for a hard tackle is **NOT** an ICR. If caught, it can get you red carded. Jumping up quickly, smiling at your opponent, acting **AS IF** you love it and playing with twice the intensity **IS** an ICR. That kind of response will definitely unnerve your opposition.

STEP #3 • Mentally practice being in a competitive situation when your hot buttons get pushed and responding with your ICRs. Sufficient mental rehearsal of ICRs will allow you to respond with them whenever your buttons get pushed under pressure.

# Making Mastery and Coping Tapes

One of the best ways to enhance the effectiveness of your mental rehearsal sessions is to use tape recordings. You can develop your own mastery or coping tapes and use them in preparation for a big game. The **FIRST** step is writing a script in the first person describing the sights, sounds, atmosphere, feelings and emotions associated with the particular performance outcome you want. For example, you might describe winning a State Championship game including all the details of the place, the people there, the opponents you beat, the exaltation, satisfaction, etc. Make that game experience so vivid you can even taste your own sweat. Select background music that will help bring you into the game experience. The dialogue and music combined should elicit strong sensory and emotional images for you.

Personally designed and narrated mastery and coping tapes are particularly powerful tools because they stimulate your own powers of visualization, often more intensely than a commercially made version. The detailed script helps structure the imagery sessions, leading you deeply into the game experience. Replaying these imagery tapes prepares you mentally and emotionally for recreating these images in reality. Directions for creating your own tapes are included in the following pages.

Since coping imagery involves correcting or rebounding from mistakes, or controlling runaway emotions, you may want to begin working with these experiences first. **NOTE: COPING TAPES SHOULD BE REPLACED BY MASTERY TAPES IN THE LAST WEEK OR TWO, OR BEFORE A BIG GAME.** You do not want the negative images from the coping tapes to interfere with your play. So days before that big game, switch to the mastery tape and let all your energy go into visualizing a strong successful performance.

The basic sequence in this coping exercise involves imagining yourself in a stressful situation and beginning to see, feel and hear things that upset you. (note: this is a 2nd strategy for coping, the 1st strategy above involved developing an Ideal Coping Response (ICR) and mentally rehearsing it). When you feel yourself losing control, you immediately apply the "Thought stopping" technique. First, you say, "Stop." Then you take one or two slow deep breaths and use key words or phrases to slow yourself down. Third, you re-frame the thought or emotion. For example, if the negative thought was, "That guy is quicker and stronger than me and I am going to get beaten", you re-frame your reaction and think, "I am as quick and strong as I need to be." Fourth, and finally, you refocus your attention and concentrate on the task at hand.

# Coping Tape Preparation

Have a pencil and a supply of paper handy for taking notes. Anticipate a stressful situation that might occur prior to, during or following a match.

# Procedure

1) Write down a list of images - sights, sounds, smells, feelings - associated with that situation.

2) Write down the negative, self-defeating, inappropriate thoughts that might occur to you in this situation.

3) Think of things you could say to yourself that would help you stop the negative thoughts and regain control. Write these down on a separate page.

4) Rephrase your negative thoughts into positive, confidence-building statements. Write down these new, helpful messages.

5) Using your notes, create a script and record it on a cassette. If you wish, choose relaxing background music to set the mood. Speaking slowly and distinctly, guide yourself through the coping experience. Remember the 5 steps for "thought stopping."

#1 Recognize the negative thought.

#2 Tell yourself, "Stop."

#3 Let go of the thought with a slow deep breath.

#4 Re-phrase the thought into a positive.

#5 Re-focus your concentration.

# Mastery Tape Preparation

Pick a big game later in the season that you want to mentally prepare for. Use the tape recording to help you use your mastery mental rehearsal. Have a pencil and a supply of paper handy for taking notes.

# Procedure

1) Imagine an upcoming match. Keeping it as realistic as possible, write down the details of the situation. Set the stage for the game by describing the weather, field conditions, crowd, sounds, your body sensations and emotions - all the sights, sounds, smells and feelings associated with this match.

2) Write down your thoughts before, during and after the game. Describe your emotions and the body sensations that you experience in this peak performance.

3) Using your notes, write out a script that guides you through all aspects of the game, starting either the night before or day of the game, and helps you experience it vividly. Keep it realistic and focus on **HOW** well you play.

4) Record the script, talking very slowly to allow yourself the time to men tally rehearse. Use different background music that helps you relax, in the beginning, and get pumped, just before and during the game.

5) Like all imagery sessions, use relaxation exercises to prepare yourself, then turn on the mastery tape to help you see and experience that perfect game in your mind's eye.

# Chapter 8 • The Principles of Peak Performance

## A Coach's and Player's Guide To Pre-Game Preparation

In **EVERY** peak performance there are certain elements that are **ALWAYS** present. These elements can serve as a **PRE-GAME** guideline to insure that you perform to the best of your abilities. When these elements are present you will play well. When they are absent your play will suffer. As a coach, following these guidelines will insure that you get the most from your players both in practice and in games. Violate these principles of peak performance and your team will continually lose games they should not lose!

**#1 FUN** • In every peak performance, the athlete is having the time of his life. He is loving what he is doing and does not want to see it end. If you want to play to your potential you **MUST** have fun **PLAYING** the game. I am **NOT** talking about the "I do not care", goof off kind of fun. I am talking about hard work, intensity and loving the challenge. If you go into your match looking forward to it you will maximize your chances of playing well.

Coaches who carry this attitude into big games keep their players loose enough to play like champions. A game should **NEVER** be presented as so big that your players can not enjoy themselves. If you are too serious about the match you will only end up tightening your team up too much. The best thing you can say to a team **BEFORE** a huge game isn't simply go out there and enjoy yourselves, but rather "You are ready, you have paid your dues, **NOW** is the time to have **FUN!**"

**#2 HIGH SELF-ESTEEM** • In peak performances the athlete likes himself. He feels good about who he is and what he can do. Self-esteem is a critically important variable in performance. You will almost always play in direct relation to how you feel about yourself. Even talented players perform far below their potential if they have low self-esteem.

As a coach, your players' level of self-esteem should be a major guideline for what you do or say with them. Anything that diminishes an athlete's self-esteem will hurt your cause and undermine your coaching efforts. Anything that enhances self-esteem in your players will insure that you get the maximum performance from them on the field. This does **NOT** mean you can not yell, be strict or set firm limits with your players. This does **NOT** mean that you can not be a disciplinarian. Many good coaches in fact are quite strict! You can be strict and criticize without decimating an athlete's self-esteem.

**#3 PROCESS, NOT OUTCOME, FOCUSED** • In the middle of a peak performance the athlete is totally oblivious to the outcome of the game. When you play well you are not thinking about winning or losing, or what will happen if you do not make this kick. Instead you are completely focused on the **HERE** and **NOW** process of the game. You are concentrating on what you are doing while you are doing it. **THE BIGGEST CAUSE OF SOCCER PLAYERS PLAYING FAR BELOW THEIR POTENTIAL IS CONCENTRATING ON THE OUTCOME OF THE MATCH, KICK OR PLAY.**

This factor is important for coaches to keep in mind when they think about pre-game and half-time talks. **YOU WILL WIN MORE WHEN YOU COACH THE PROCESS, NOT THE OUTCOME.** The more you get your players focusing on the importance of a match, what is at stake and what will happen if they play poorly, the greater chance there is that your team will tighten up and bomb. Winning is a paradox. You get to it by **NOT** coaching it. Focus your players on what they have to do at that moment, on their individual jobs, on each play. When you can accomplish this re-focusing, winning will take care of itself.

**#4 FREE TO FAIL OR MAKE MISTAKES** • In the middle of a peak performance the athlete is totally oblivious to making mistakes or failing. When mistakes happen, the athlete quickly lets them go and mentally returns to the task at hand. Athletes who are afraid to make mistakes or fail are tentative and play poorly. Play as if you have nothing to lose and let your mistakes go! Remember, concentrate on what you **WANT** to happen, **NOT** what you are **AFRAID** will happen.

Coaches who create an atmosphere in which players are free to fail will produce peak performers. If your players know it is **OK** to fail they will be more relaxed and take more risks for you. **THE VERY WORST THING A COACH CAN TEACH AN ATHLETE IS THAT MISTAKES AND FAILING ARE BAD AND CAUSE FOR HUMILIATION.** Punish or humiliate your athletes when they mess up and you will not only turn them into self-conscious, overly cautious underachievers, **BUT** you will also make them lose all respect for you. Teach them to go for it. Teach them that failing or losing is a necessary stepping stone to becoming a winner!

**#5 CHALLENGE, DO NOT THREATEN** • The athlete who recalls a past peak performance talks about rising to meet a challenge. Whether the challenge came from within or without does not matter. Inwardly the player responds to an internal "I know I can!" Challenging yourself to go beyond your limits is one of the **BEST** ways to motivate yourself. Threatening yourself is one of the worst.

Many coaches use threats to try to motivate their players to peak performance. A threat entails future punishment or the loss of something important.

For example, "If you don't make THIS kick you don't belong on this team" or "If you guys don't win this game, I am going to sit you ALL out for the next two and let the freshmen play!"

Threats engender fear, produce excess muscle tension and **DISTRACT** the player from the game. Certainly fear is a powerful motivator, but you must know **HOW** to use it. More often than not fear shuts an athlete down rather than empowering him to great performances. Threats have no place in your pre-game talk **UNLESS** you know for a fact that your team is under aroused or "not enough nervous."

### #6 AUTOMATIC - EFFORTLESS - NON THINKING • When you play your very best you are **NOT THINKING** about what you are doing, you are just doing it! You are playing tough and hard, but playing with "effortless effort". There is an easy, automatic quality to your play. This is what I call a "game mentality." Once you have learned a skill, your best performances come from your unconscious. That is, you do not think about the skill anymore, you just allow yourself to do it automatically.

This is in sharp contrast to your worst games where nothing comes easily and you have a tendency to **THINK TOO** much and **TRY TOO HARD**. You evaluate your play, criticize your mistakes and coach yourself too much. This is what I call a "practice mentality." When you are first learning a skill or strategy it is important to think about it and self-consciously evaluate how you are performing. The skill does not come easily so there is a tendency to force your body to do what it is supposed to.

Peak performance is about putting yourself on automatic and using a let-it-happen "game mentality." In other words, game time is time to **TRUST** yourself, your abilities and training. **YOU CAN NOT FORCE YOURSELF TO PLAY WELL, YOU HAVE TO LET IT HAPPEN**. When athletes think too much about the importance of playing well, they begin thinking too much and trying too hard. **TRYING TOO HARD IS THE GAME OF DIMINISHING RETURNS**. The harder you try to do well, the worse you do!

As a coach it is important for you to understand this distinction between a game and practice mentality. You do not want your players in a practice mentality during games. You do not want them consciously thinking about mechanics and what they should do. You want them responding the way they have been trained. That is, you want them in a "game mentality", trusting that it is all there and just letting their skills come out.

This means that the less you get them to focus on pre-game and half-time the better. Too many coaches are guilty of over coaching, of trying to cram too much information in just before the game. The last thing you want to do with your players is put too much in their heads. Give them one or two important focal points for the match and encourage them to **TRUST** and **LET IT HAPPEN**.

**#7 MENTALLY AND PHYSICALLY RELAXED** • Without being mentally and physically relaxed you can not learn effectively nor play to your potential. You have to be able to master the pressure of competition in order to have peak performances. If you can not handle your pre-game nerves, it is critical that you invest consistent time training yourself in arousal control techniques. The foundation of your mental toughness lies in this ability to control your levels of stress. Turn to the chapter on stress and performance for the specifics.

As a coach **IT IS** imperative that you understand the relationship between stress and performance and know what to do when your athletes are under or over-aroused before a game. Adding this knowledge and these strategies to your coaching repertoire will make you a more effective and successful teacher.

# Conclusion

There is a mental toughness myth that exists in many sports. This myth claims that you are either born with a "good head" or you are not. That is, there is very little you can do about improving your ability to handle pressure or control your emotions because this is just how you are. Basically it is saying, if you are a head case now, you will **ALWAYS** be a head case. This myth, like most, is also false.

With patience, a little hard work and consistent practice you can train yourself to develop the mind of a champion. Mental toughness can be learned! You can do it! This book provides you with all the strategies you need to become a mentally tough soccer player.

Remember, if you have a dream to go as far as possible in this sport, you have to train your mind as well as your body. Great soccer players do not leave the mental side of their performance to chance. This is why they always seem to come through regardless of the odds against them or the pressure of the moment.

Start right now to train yourself to systematically think and act like a champion! Use this book as a tool. Mental training, like physical training, is an ongoing process. You have to continually work at all aspects of your game to establish and maintain the competitive advantage.

Which of the exercises and ideas in this book work for you is really **NOT** important. What **IS** important is finding those strategies that fit you as an individual and **USING** them. Some of these you may have developed on your own without any conscious awareness. Others you can take an active role in developing.

If I can help you with any part of your mental training please feel free to call or write. My goal is to provide clear, helpful information, and I would be happy to help you with any issues or problems that come up for you in the course of your training.

88 Wells Road • Spring City Pennsylvania 19475

1-800-331-5191 • www.reedswain.com